The Past in Question
Series Editor: *J. F. Aylett*

Life in Elizabethan Times

David Whitehall

Hodder & Stoughton
LONDON SYDNEY AUCKLAND TORONTO

Acknowledgements

The publishers would like to thank the following for their permission to reproduce copyright photographs and cartoons: Blairs College, Aberdeen 28 (top); The British Library 4 (top) 27, 38; Reproduced by Courtesy of the Trustees of the British Museum 40, 41 (lower); The Courtauld Institute of Art 5 (left); Edinburgh University Library 34 (top), 46 (all), 47; The Trustees of the Ellesmere 1939 Settlement 45; Mary Evans Picture Library 11, 12, 19 (top/middle), 26 (top), 34 (lower), 37 (left); Fotomas Index 16 (left), 17, 36 (left); Photographie Giraudon 15; The Duke of Hamilton, Lennoxlove, Haddington 29; History Today 16 (right); The Hulton-Deutsch Collection 14, 18 (top), 23 (left), 44 (left); The Illustrated London News Picture Library 31; The Mansell Collection 18 (lower), 19 (lower), 23 (right), 24, 42, 43 (left), 44 (right); Reproduced by permission of the Marquess of Bath, Longleat House, Warminster, Wiltshire 22 and cover; National Galleries of Scotland 10, 28 (lower); National Portrait Gallery, London 7, 13; Plymouth City Museums and Art Gallery 21, 32; The Tate Gallery 8 (right); Reproduced by permission of the Trustees, The Wallace Collection, London 8 (left); By Courtesy of the Dean and Chapter of Westminster 5 (right).

For my parents
Illustrations by Philip Page

© 1990 David Whitehall

First published 1990

British Library Cataloguing in Publication Data

Whitehall, David
 Life in Elizabethan times. – (The past in question).
 1. England. Social life, 1558–1603
 I. Title II. Series
 942.05'5

 ISBN 0-340-50262-2

All rights reserved. No part of this publication may be reproduced or transmitted in any form or by any means, electronic or mechanical, including photocopying, recording, or any information storage and retrieval system, without permission in writing from the publisher or under licence from the Copyright Licensing Agency Limited. Further details of such licences (for reprographic reproduction) may be obtained from the Copyright Licensing Agency Limited, of 33–34 Alfred Place, London WC1E 7DP.

Typeset in 12 on 13pt Century Schoolbook by Keyset Composition, Colchester.
Printed in Great Britain for the educational publishing division of Hodder and Stoughton Limited, Mill Road, Dunton Green, Sevenoaks, Kent by St Edmundsbury Press Limited, Bury St Edmunds, Suffolk.

Contents

1	Elizabeth I, 1533–1603	4
2	The Religious Problem, 1559	6
3	The Mysterious Death of Amy Dudley	8
4	Royal Murder in Scotland	10
5	The Northern Rebellion, 1569	12
6	Catholics and Protestants	16
7	How Farming Changed in Elizabethan Times	18
8	A Farm Worker's Life	20
9	Growing Up in Elizabethan Times	22
10	Captain John Hawkins: Trader or Pirate?	24
11	Women in Elizabethan Times	26
12	Mary, Queen of Scots	28
13	The Spanish Armada, 1588	30
14	Sport and Entertainment	34
15	Dealing with the Poor	36
16	Virginia, England's First Colony	38
17	Superstition and Witchcraft	42
18	The Essex Rebellion, 1601	44
19	Ireland	46
	Glossary	48
	Index	48

1 Elizabeth I, 1533–1603

A *This drawing of 1589 shows an Elizabethan progress.*

B *A portrait of Queen Elizabeth by Franciscus Hogenburg, between 1568–9.*

On 18 November 1558, church bells rang in the villages and towns. Queen Mary I was dead. She had been an unpopular queen and in London people danced in the streets. Now they had high hopes of her half-sister Elizabeth, the new queen of England.

Elizabeth was 25. She was queen for the next 45 years and in that time England became rich and powerful. However, in 1558 she had many problems to solve.

Some people said that Elizabeth had no right to be queen. Instead they wanted her cousin Mary, Queen of Scots. There were serious arguments between Protestants and Catholics. Each wanted their own form of Christianity to be the only religion in England.

War with France made things worse, and there was not enough money to pay for the army and navy.

Elizabeth knew that she had to get people on her side. She did this by going round the country and speaking to as many people as possible. Whether they were rich or poor did not matter to her. If they liked her, they would obey her.

The journeys that the Queen made were called progresses. During one of them a farmer stepped out from the crowd waiting to see Elizabeth and stopped her coach. He shouted out that he wanted to speak to the Queen. Instead of being angry, Elizabeth laughed and let him kiss her hand. The crowd loved it.

For those people who couldn't get to see her, the Queen made sure they could see her picture — in bibles, for example. But by studying these pictures today, it is difficult to decide what she looked like. Even her painters could not agree.

Most of them tried to show the Queen at her best. They became rich and famous for doing so. They also knew that if Elizabeth disliked a picture she would have it destroyed.

Painters who did not paint her in the way she wanted, found it hard to get work in the future. Because of this they did not always show what she really looked like.

In this chapter you will see how important it is to check the date of any source — to check *when* a picture was painted, or *when* a letter was written.

C *An order issued by Lord Cecil, advisor to the Queen in about 1570.*

Many painters have done portraits of the Queen but none has sufficiently shown her looks and charms. Therefore Her Majesty commands all manner of persons to stop doing portraits of her until a clever painter has finished one which all other painters can copy. Her Majesty in the meantime forbids the showing of any portraits which are ugly, until they are improved.

D *The Rainbow Portrait of Queen Elizabeth by an unknown artist.*

E *This description of Elizabeth is taken from a letter written by André Hurault de Maisse, French ambassador, 1597:*

As for her face it is long and thin and appears to be very aged. Her teeth are very yellow and decayed.

F *A description of Elizabeth written by a German writer, Paul Hentzner in 1597:*

Her face oblong, fair but wrinkled. Her eyes small, yet black and pleasant. Her nose is a little hooked, her lips narrow. Her hair is an auburn colour, but false.

G *Thomas Platter wrote this description of Elizabeth in 1599:*

Although she was already 74, she was very youthful in appearance, seeming no more than 20 years of age.

H *Tomb portrait by Maximilian Colt, 1605, almost certainly carved from Queen Elizabeth's death mask.*

Activities

1. a) Look at source D. Write out the five words which you think best describe Elizabeth: proud, intelligent, fat, honest, ugly, shy, attractive, young, thin, brave, pretty, confident, plain, smart, old, cruel, weak, cowardly, powerful, trustworthy, unattractive. Give reasons for your choices.
   b) Look at source B. Which five words best describe this impression of the Queen?
   c) Which written source agrees with source D? Explain why.
   d) Do you think source D was painted before 1570, or after it? Explain why you think this.

2. a) Read sources E and F. Compare these descriptions of Elizabeth with source B. How are they different?
   b) Suggest a reason for the differences.

3. a) Read source C. How did Elizabeth control the way she looked in paintings?
   b) Why do you think she did this?

4. Which sources do you think are likely to give accurate evidence about Elizabeth? Explain why.

2 The Religious Problem, 1559

When Elizabeth became Queen, her first job was to solve the problem of religion. For people living then, religion was a very important part of their lives. The trouble was they could not agree about it.

Mary I had been a Catholic. She thought her form of Christianity was the only true one and any priest who said differently was punished. Many were burnt to death.

But Elizabeth, like many people in England, was Protestant. What annoyed her about the Catholics was their views on the Pope. They thought he was more important than any king or queen. Whatever the Pope said, they had to obey.

Mary I accepted this and never went against his wishes. Queen Elizabeth wanted to rule the country without interference from anyone. So in 1559 she made herself Head of the Church in England. She made all the churches Protestant, instead of Catholic. From now on, everyone had to obey her before anyone else.

Unfortunately this was not the end of the problem. England was at war with France. Most French people were Catholic and their King, Henry II, chose this moment to send an army of soldiers to Scotland. Here they waited to invade England. They were there to help Elizabeth's cousin Mary, Queen of Scots, who was a Catholic.

Henry planned to get rid of Elizabeth and put Mary in her place. She would rule with his advice, and make England a Catholic country again.

Help for Elizabeth came from King Philip II of Spain. He warned Henry that if French soldiers invaded England, Spain would attack France.

Philip, like most people in Spain and Portugal, was Catholic, but he wanted to give Elizabeth time. He thought she might change her mind and become a Catholic after all.

Spain was the most powerful country in Europe. For the next few years Elizabeth was careful not to annoy King Philip or the Catholics living in England. All she asked of them was that they attend church services.

For Elizabeth these were a useful way of getting her message across. She made sure that priests reminded people that she was Head of the Church.

A *This map shows part of Western Europe in 1559.*

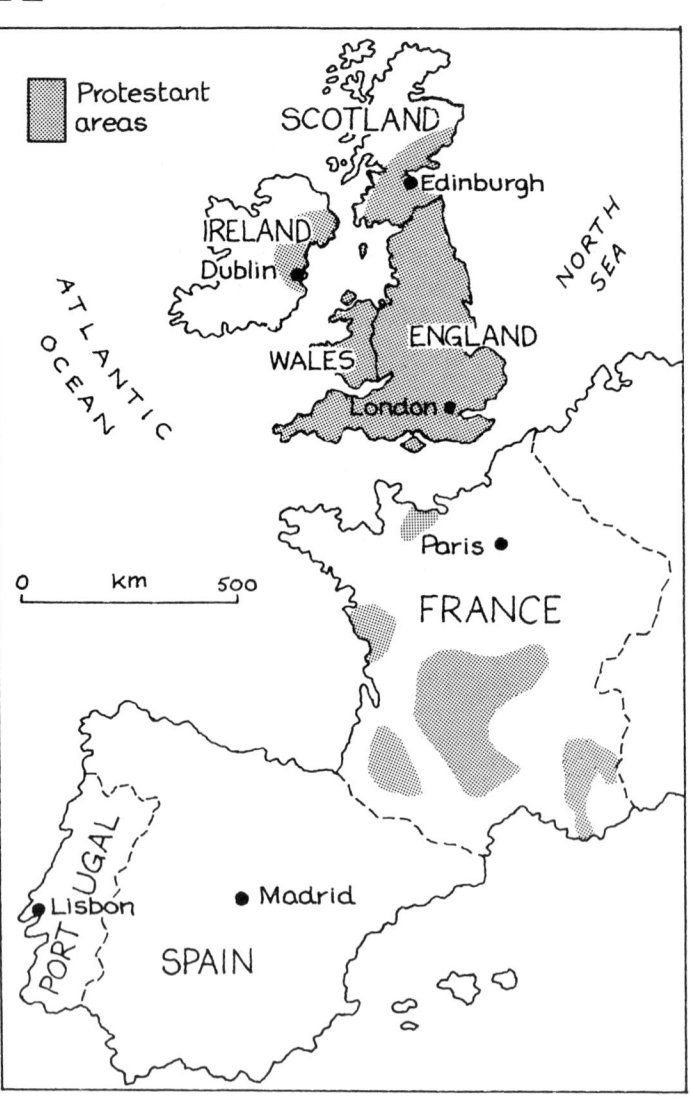

B *Religious differences between Protestants (left) and Catholics (right).*

C *A day in the life of a **Puritan** lady, taken from the diary of Lady Margaret Hoby, 1599–1605.*

In the morning after private prayers I wrote some notes in my **Testament** till 10 o'clock. Then I went for a walk. After I returned home I prayed, read a chapter of the Bible and embroidered till dinner time. I did some things about the house till four. Then I wrote out the sermon which I had heard in church the day before, and returned to prayer.

I walked till supper time and thought about what I had read. I asked God to pardon me for my sins, though I knew I was guilty and went to bed.

D *A priest's complaint written in 1603:*

As for my parishioners, they are the kind of people that love a pot of ale better than a **pulpit**, and a corn rick better than a church door. They come to church services more out of fashion than devotion. They are happy after a little kneeling, coughing and spitting to help me sing out a psalm and sleep at the second lesson. They wake up to say Amen and stay until the clerk has mentioned the latest stray bullock, black sheep or grey mare. Then they are glad to get home for dinner.

E *Mary, Queen of Scots, painted in 1578 by an unknown artist.*

Activities

1. a) Copy the pictures which show the differences between Protestants and Catholics in your book.
   b) Below are various statements about Protestants and Catholics in Elizabethan times. Write each statement under whichever picture it fits: The Catholics believed the Pope was the Head of the Church; Protestant priests could marry; the Catholic prayer book was written in Latin; Protestants confessed their sins directly to God; Catholic priests could not marry; Protestants believed their king or queen was Head of the Church; Catholics confessed their sins to a priest who forgave them on God's behalf; the Protestant prayer book was written in English.

2. a) What problems did King Henry II of France and King Philip II of Spain cause Elizabeth?
   b) Copy the map into your book. Draw a key to it and shade in the Protestant and Catholic countries mentioned in this chapter.

3. Read sources C and D. You are Lady Hoby and have just attended the church service described in source D. Write a letter to a Puritan friend and describe the behaviour of the other church-goers. Make it clear how you think they should behave on Sundays.

3 The Mysterious Death of Amy Dudley

On 7 September 1560, Queen Elizabeth returned to her palace at Windsor after a morning's hunting. With her was Lord Robert Dudley. He was 28 years old, tall and handsome.

A *A painting of Lord Dudley by Steven van der Meulen, about 1565.*

Some people said they were lovers and that Lord Dudley wanted to marry Elizabeth. This would make him King, and the most powerful man in England.

If this was Lord Dudley's plan, he had a problem. He was already married although his wife Amy did not see much of him. She lived at Cumnor Place, the home of family friends. He spent much of his time away from home, and usually stayed at the Queen's palace.

On the morning of 8 September, Amy Dudley and her friend Mrs Owen were alone in the house. Their servants had the day off and had gone to a fair nearby. When they returned to Cumnor Place four hours later, they found Amy lying in the hall at the bottom of the stairs — dead.

Her neck was broken. There were no other marks on her body — no cuts or bruises and nothing to suggest that Amy had tried to struggle before she died. The staircase was not steep and each step was wide and low. There should have been enough room for Amy to stop herself from falling.

Historians do not know for certain how she died. There is not enough evidence. Unfortunately for historians this is often the case.

There are several **theories** about the death of Amy Dudley. It looked at first as if it was an accident. Amy had lost her balance and tripped

B *A 19th-century painting which shows Amy lying dead.*

while walking down the stairs. Later, people wondered whether Lord Dudley or even Elizabeth might have had something to do with her death.

Two weeks after she died, Amy was buried in St Mary's Church, Oxford. Her grave has long since been dug over so there is no hope of doctors today being able to examine her remains.

Now, as then, Amy's death is a mystery.

C *This is part of a letter written by the Spanish ambassador, Conde de Feria in April 1559. He was a Catholic.*

It is said that Her Majesty visits Lord Dudley in his room day and night. People go so far as to say that his wife has a sickness in one of her breasts. And that the Queen is only waiting for her to die to marry Lord Robert.

D *In August 1560, de Quadra, the new Spanish ambassador, described what Lord Cecil had told him.*

They were thinking of destroying Lord Robert's wife. They said that she was ill but she was not ill at all. She was very well and taking care not to be poisoned.

E *On 10 September 1560 Amy's maid, Mrs Pirto, was asked how she thought Amy had died.*

By my faith I think it was an accident. It wasn't done by any man or by herself for she was a good woman. Every day she would pray upon her knees and asked God to save her from her desperation.

F *This theory about Amy's death was written by Ian Aird in 1956.*

A doctor today, called to see a patient found with a broken neck at the bottom of a stair-case, would suspect a **spontaneous fracture** of the spine. This kind of fracture was not known to most Elizabethan doctors. It occurs when the spine, weakened by disease or age, breaks under the strain of normal movement.

If the neck bones did break, the patient would collapse paralysed from the neck down — and might die suddenly. This kind of fracture is more likely to occur in stepping downstairs than walking on the level.

In a woman of Amy's age (28), the likeliest cause of a spontaneous fracture of the spine would be breast cancer.

G *These pictures show possible explanations for Amy's death.*

Activities

1 a) What reason did Lord Dudley have to murder his wife?
   b) Which source supports the theory that Amy was murdered? Give reasons.

2 a) Read source C. What impression do you get of Queen Elizabeth from this source? Explain your answer.
   b) Why might this writer not give a fair picture of the Queen?

3 a) Can you think of any reason why Amy would commit suicide? Explain your answer.
   b) Is there any source which supports the theory of suicide? Explain your answer.
   c) What facts about her death do not support this theory?

4 a) Read source F. How did Amy die according to this writer?
   b) What evidence is there in the other sources to support this theory?

5 a) Make a list of the people you would want to interview about Amy's death.
   b) What questions would you ask them?

4 Royal Murder in Scotland

While Elizabeth was Queen of England, Scotland was a separate country with its own ruler, Mary, Queen of Scots. In July 1565 Mary married Lord Henry Darnley. From the start the marriage was an unhappy one and soon Mary and Lord Darnley fell out. There were rumours about Mary's friendship with David Rizzio, an Italian musician. Mary was pregnant and some people said that he, and not Lord Darnley, was the father.

On the evening of Saturday 9 March, the Queen held a supper party at Holyrood Palace in Edinburgh. The party was held in a small room next to Mary's bedroom. In here a **tapestry** hid a private stair-case which led to Lord Darnley's room on the ground floor.

A *In his book,* Queen Mary of Scotland and the Islands *(1935), Stefan Zweig described what happened next:*

> There was no sign of anything unusual — until the tapestry was pulled aside and Darnley entered the room. The tapestry was lifted again. This time the newcomer was Patrick, Lord Ruthven. He had a sword in his hand. The Queen was instantly worried, for no one but her husband was allowed to use the private stair-case. Ruthven said, 'There is no harm intended to anyone but that coward David.' Mary said to the intruder, 'What has he done?' Ruthven replied, 'Ask the King, your husband, Madam.'
>
> Mary turned to Darnley but shiftily he turned his eyes away and said, 'I know nothing of this matter.'
>
> Now more heavy footsteps were heard behind the tapestry. One after another the conspirators formed a wall to block Rizzio's escape. Ruthven advanced towards him as another of the conspirators threw a rope over the Italian's shoulders and began to drag him away. In the confusion, the supper table was overturned and the candles went out.
>
> Rizzio hung on to the Queen's dress crying in terror. Another man pressed a loaded pistol against Mary's side, while the murderers hurried the shrieking Rizzio out of the supper room.
>
> As they dragged him through the bedroom, he clung on to the bedclothes still crying to the Queen for help. The **assassins** clubbed his fingers to make him let go. Then they stabbed him savagely and flung his **mutilated** body through an open window into the courtyard below.

B *This 19th-century painting by William Allen shows the murder of David Rizzio.*

Within days of the murder, Mary and Lord Darnley seemed to be friends again. Then, in November 1566 Mary met with some of her nobles. Amongst them was the Earl of Bothwell, who was rumoured to be the Queen's lover. She told the nobles she was unhappy with Lord Darnley. They suggested ways Mary could be rid of the problem. Divorce was one possibility. Murder was another.

In January 1567 Lord Darnley was recovering from illness. He was staying at a house in Kirk o' Field, just outside Edinburgh.

On 5 and 6 February, Mary stayed with Lord Darnley, sleeping in a room below his. She

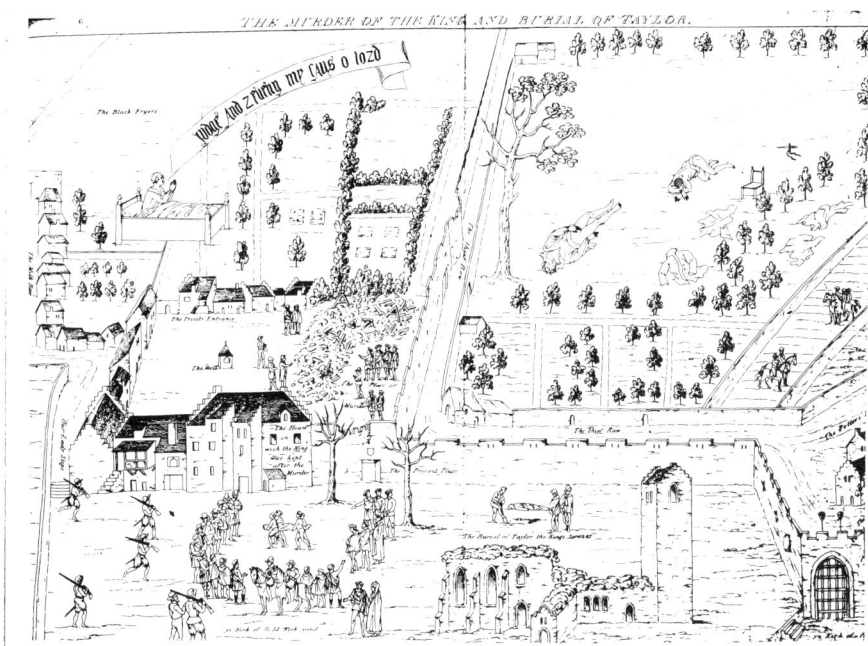

visited him again on the following Sunday evening with the Earl of Bothwell and three other nobles. They left at about midnight to attend a wedding party at Holyrood Palace.

Two hours later Lord Darnley was dead.

E *This is a print of Kirk o' Field sketched by an unknown artist, 10 February 1567.*

C *The Earl of Lennox, Lord Darnley's father, wrote this account between 21–26 May, 1568.*

The King had been asleep for about an hour when 50 people surrounded the house. Sixteen of them, Bothwell being the chief, came the secret way she had used to visit the King. They found the King in bed and suffocated him with a napkin soaked in vinegar. Then they took his body into the garden and lay beside him his night gown. Next to him they laid his servant, William Taylor who had died in the same way. When this was finished, the house was blown up. When the Queen heard the noise of the explosion, she went to bed.

D *This extract is from a **ballad** published by an unknown writer in London between 1579 and 1599.*

When he came into the chamber the **page** began to tell,
'You are betrayed O Noble King for powder I do smell,
Flee from here, haste you away and I on you will wait.'
The King hearing this leapt out of the window straight.
But one stood under the window and took him by his arm
Saying, 'O man fear not, for you will not be harmed.'
Two more took the King and tied his feet and hands.
On a pear tree in an orchard this noble King was hanged.

Historians do not know whether Mary was involved in the plot to kill Lord Darnley. Three months after his death she married the Earl of Bothwell.

Activities

1. a) In source A, what evidence suggests that Darnley knew about the plot to kill Rizzio?
   b) Mary was six months pregnant. Is there any evidence to suggest the conspirators meant to harm her unborn child?
   c) Why might they try to do this?
   d) List five sounds you might have heard during the attack on Rizzio. Use source A to help you.

2. Look at source E and describe what you think it shows.

3. Compare source C with source D. List three ways in which their accounts of Lord Darnley's murder are different.
   b) Which source do you think provides the most reliable evidence about Lord Darnley's murder? Explain why you think this.

5 The Northern Rebellion, 1569

A *Durham Cathedral.*

B *A royal footsoldier and a rebel horseman as drawn by a modern artist.*

On 14 November 1569, 300 armed horsemen galloped through the streets of Durham. They stopped outside the cathedral, one of the oldest churches in England, then smashed down its doors.

Once inside, they grabbed the Protestant prayer books and bibles and burned them in a huge bonfire. The Northern Rebellion had started.

The men were led by the Catholic Earls of Westmorland and Northumberland. The year before, Mary, Queen of Scots had been forced to flee to England. According to rumours, the earls wanted to get rid of Elizabeth and make Mary the new Catholic Queen of England.

Meanwhile Mary had to stay at Tutbury Castle in Staffordshire. Elizabeth thought it was too dangerous to let her out. People wondered if the earls would use their army to try to set her free.

On 15 November, the rebel army marched to Darlington. The next day it was in Richmond, then Ripon. With their 4000 footsoldiers and 1600 horsemen, the earls controlled most of Yorkshire and County Durham. At this rate they would reach Tutbury and Mary, Queen of Scots in four days.

In York the royal army of Lord Sussex had only 400 horsemen and 1500 footsoldiers. Many of these were farmworkers who had never been trained to fight. Lord Warwick had promised to help by sending 10,000 soldiers from the south of England. But they would not arrive for at least another week.

At this point, if you were Queen Elizabeth, what would you do next?

1. Order Lord Sussex to march his army out of York and fight the rebels.
2. Tell Lord Sussex to follow the rebel army at a distance but order him not to fight.
3. Move Mary, Queen of Scots to a castle further south.
4. Order Lord Sussex to wait in York until the southern army arrived.

Before you decide, read source C.

C *This extract is from a letter written by Sir Ralph Sadler on 6 December 1569.*

Her Majesty knows that her army in Yorkshire will not increase and be able to match the rebels. It is easy to find the reason. The people are totally blinded with the old **Popish** religion. They are in favour of the rebels and although they are here with us in person, their hearts are with them. If we should go to battle with this northern force they would fight faintly. For if the father be on this side, the son is on the other, and one brother with us and the other with the rebels.

D *A 19th-century engraving of the Earl of Westmorland.*

E *The Proclamation of the Earls, 16 November, 1569.*

Thomas, Earl of Northumberland and Charles, Earl of Westmorland, the Queen's most true and lawful **subjects** send greetings.

In the last twelve years certain nobles have set up and maintained a new religion. To put this right, some foreign countries intend soon to invade this country. This will be to our utter destruction. So we are now forced to change it ourselves. If we do not do this, we will all be made slaves to them. Therefore we require you to do your duty to God and set forth the true, Catholic religion. Come and join us quickly with all the armour you have. God save the Queen.

F *This extract is from a letter written by the Spanish Ambassador.*

On the 22 September 1569, a servant of the Duke of Northumberland, whom I knew, came to visit me. He made me the sign which his master and I had agreed upon. He said that his lord and his friends in the north had agreed to free the Queen of Scotland. By doing this they would assure the Catholic religion and return to friendship and **alliance** with your Majesty which they want so much. They only ask that after they have released the Queen they should be aided by your Majesty with a small number of **harquebussiers**.

Activities

1. a) Describe the weapons of the footsoldier and the horseman.
   b) What advantages would the horseman have?

2. Read source C. Why does this writer think that the royal army should not fight the rebels?

3. a) According to source E, why did the nobles rebel?
   b) Why do you think the nobles didn't mention their plan to free Mary, Queen of Scots?

4. a) Read source F. To whom was this letter written?
   b) Why do you think he wrote this letter?
   c) Why might the earls want this letter kept secret? Explain your answer.

The rebellion fails

A *A map of the area of the Northern Rebellion.*

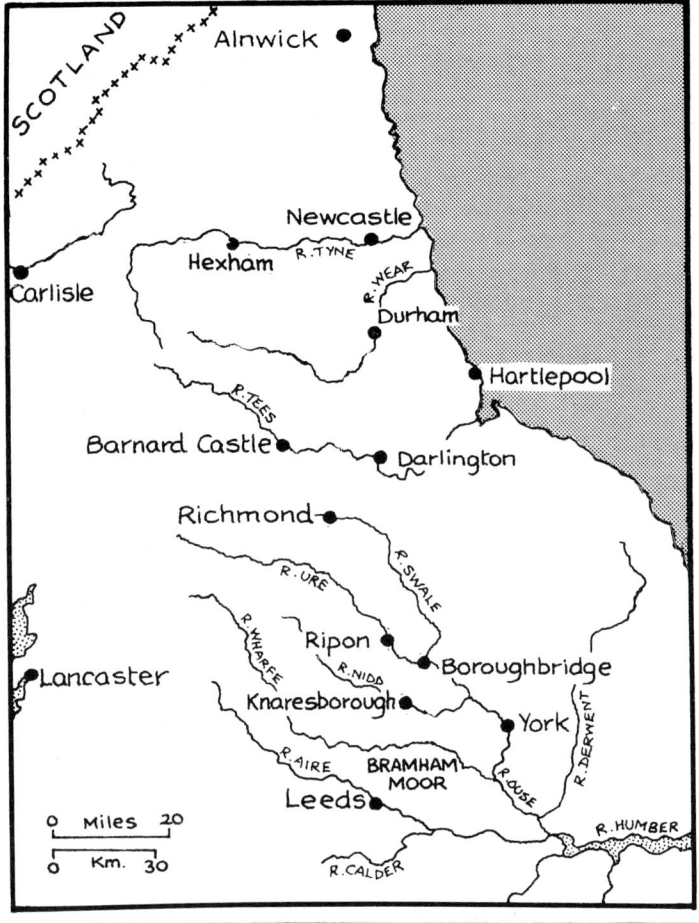

The earls continued south to Bramham Moor. Here they stayed for a week, hoping that Catholics in Lancashire and Cheshire would join them. Fortunately for Elizabeth none did, and the rebel army turned back.

It was December and the soldiers were tired and cold. Many were annoyed that they had not been paid and went home.

What was left of the rebel army marched north to Barnard Castle. This was the home of Sir George Bowes, one of Elizabeth's most loyal supporters.

For ten days the rebels besieged the castle. Inside, people were near to starvation and on 14 December they surrendered. 200 men leaped over the walls to join the rebel army. It was their last victory.

Soon after, the rebels fled to Durham. Royal soldiers from the south had at last reached Lord Sussex. Now they chased after the rebels first to Hexham, then to Carlisle. It was too late. The earls had escaped to Liddesdale across the Scottish border.

From here the Earl of Westmorland sailed to the Netherlands. For the next thirty years he worked for the King of Spain helping him with his plans to invade England. He died an old man in 1601.

B *This **woodcut** shows Catholics plotting against the Queen and, on the right, the Earl of Northumberland's execution.*

The Earl of Northumberland was not as lucky. At first he was looked after by the Lord Regent of Scotland. But only until Queen Elizabeth offered him a ransom of £2000.

As soon as it was paid, he handed the earl over to the royal soldiers. He was found guilty of treason and beheaded at York.

In the weeks that followed hundreds of rebel soldiers were caught and rounded up. Some of them were pardoned. They were set free on condition that they gave all their land to the Queen. The others were executed. Elizabeth wanted them to be an example to the people of the north. Never again would they dare to oppose her.

C *This 19th-century account describes the execution of Christopher Norton, one of the rebel leaders.*

He watched the **quartering** and death of his uncle. He knew that he himself would follow the same way and seemed very **repentant**. When he was asked whether he had offended God and the Queen, he said that he deserved to die. He pleaded with God and with all men to forgive him. Then he desired the people to pray with him.

After he had been hung for a while, and then cut down, the butcher opened him. As his insides were taken from him he cried, 'Oh Lord, Lord have mercy upon me.' And so he gave up the ghost.

D *Lord Sussex had to select rebels for execution in York. He could not decide on the men in this list. So in March 1570 he wrote to the Queen for advice.*

1. *Henry Johnson* — He is very simple and has been badly treated by his wife. When he married he agreed that if he died, she would receive his lands. So, by the law, if his life is spared the Queen shall have them. But by his death his wife shall presently have his lands.
2. *John Markenfeld* — Is very young, under twenty and has no land.
3. *Robert Lambert* — He was taken by the rebels out of his bed by force from his father-in-law's house. He had gone there intending to join Her Majesty's army, but stayed with the rebels. He has many children and is well known for his honest behaviour before this offence.
4. *Rauf Conyers* — He was servant to the Earl of Westmorland. He is of good religion and yet he followed his master in this affair. He speaks honestly and his neighbours are very sorry for him. The Queen will lose by his death.

E *Many of the rebels were executed in front of crowds of people.*

Activities

1. a) Copy the map into your book.
   b) Draw on it the route of the rebel army during the Northern Rebellion.

2. a) Look at source E and describe what you think is happening.
   b) Why do you think people were allowed to watch the rebels being executed like this?

3. a) What impression do you get of Christopher Norton from source C?
   b) This source is taken from a book written in 1840. Does this make the source useless as evidence? Give reasons for your answer.

4. You are Queen Elizabeth. Read source D, then write a letter to Lord Sussex listing the men you want executed, and those you will pardon. Make sure you fully explain your reasons.

6 Catholics and Protestants

A *The Pope excommunicates Queen Elizabeth.*

B *In February 1570 the Pope gave this order.*

> This woman, having seized the crown and monstrously taken the place of the Head of the Church of England, has reduced this kingdom to a miserable ruin.
>
> Therefore we declare that Elizabeth has incurred the sentence of excommunication. We also declare that the people of this country who have sworn an **oath** to her are freed from any duty of obedience. We command that they do not dare to obey her orders and laws. Those who do, will be included in the sentence of excommunication.

C *A picture of the Pope, and alongside it, a Catholic Cardinal. Now turn them upside down to see two more pictures. The words in each picture are translated underneath.*

After the Northern Rebellion, Queen Elizabeth wondered if there would be more plots against her. All Catholics were under suspicion and the laws against them were tightened up.

It was especially dangerous to be a Catholic priest. In the north of England they had encouraged people to rebel against Elizabeth. Now all Catholic priests were said to be guilty of **treason**. So too were people who allowed them into their homes. The punishment for treason was death.

Some Catholics built priest holes under the floor of their house. Here priests could hide if the house was searched.

In 1570 the Pope **excommunicated** Elizabeth. According to the Pope, she could no longer be Queen because she was not a Catholic and did not believe in the one, true religion. When she died she would go to hell, with all the people who had ever obeyed her.

An evil church has the face of a devil.

Sometimes wise men, sometimes foolish.

Although most English Catholics stayed loyal to the Queen, some still plotted to get rid of her. They asked Elizabeth's enemies in France and Spain to help them. These were Catholic countries. Their people soon found out how

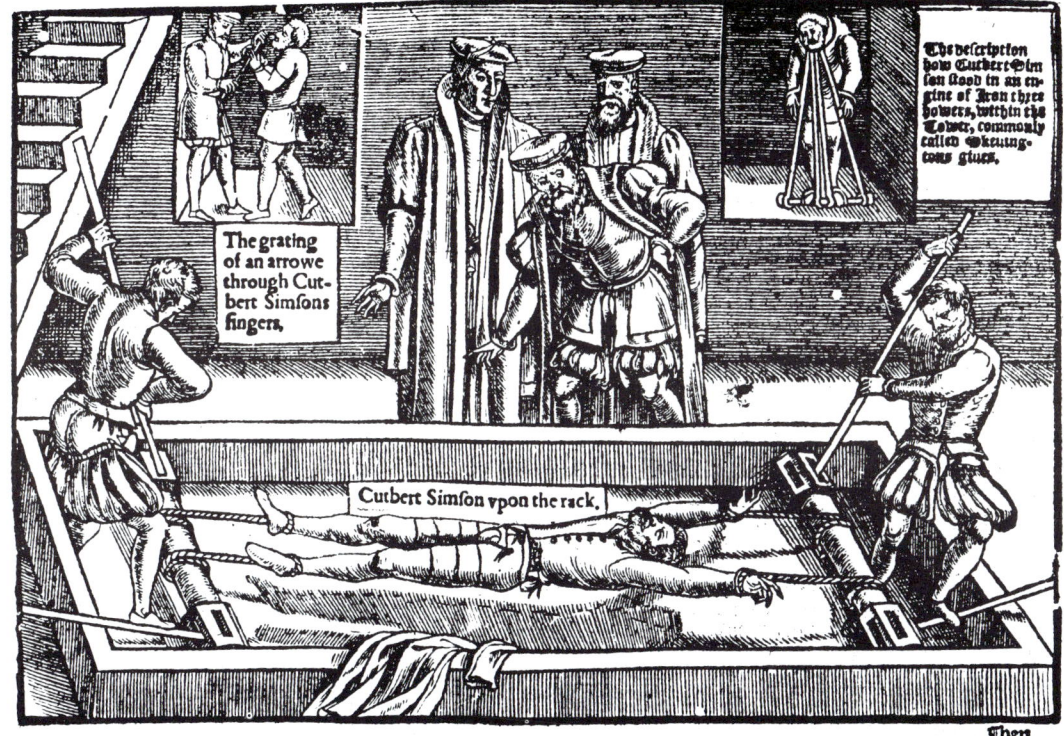

D *This engraving shows the torture of a Protestant by Catholics. It is taken from the 'Book of Martyrs' by John Foxe, published in 1563.*

Catholics in England were being treated.

They had pictures to show them — usually etchings or woodcuts. These showed Catholics being tortured in different ways by Protestants. In all the pictures the message was the same. Because of their different ideas on religion, Catholics could expect only cruelty from Protestants.

What artists in France and Spain did not show was Protestants being tortured in *their* countries. They ignored other facts too. At this time most Catholics and Protestants actually lived quite peacefully together in England. Their pictures did not show this.

French and Spanish artists showed only one side of the story. This was also true of Protestant artists in England. Their pictures poked fun at the Pope. Others made him look ugly and frightening. They were always unfair.

These artists thought that Catholic ideas on religion were wrong. Through their pictures they tried to make other people believe this too. However, not all the events which they showed actually took place. This is why historians have to check their sources very carefully.

With a picture, as with any source, they start by checking its date. The next question to ask is: who painted it? In Elizabethan times there were reasons why a Catholic or Protestant artist might not show the whole truth.

Activities

1. a) Describe the three methods of torture shown in source D.
   b) Do you think John Foxe was a Protestant, or a Catholic? Explain how you decided.

2. a) Look at source C. Do you think these pictures were done by a Protestant or a Catholic? Give reasons for your answer.
   b) What impression does source C give of this form of Christianity?

3. a) Read source B. Make a list of the words or phrases which you think give a bad impression of Queen Elizabeth.
   b) Do you think the Pope's order would make it more difficult or less difficult for Catholics to live in England? Explain your answer.

7 How Farming Changed in Elizabethan Times

A *Cutting the corn.*

When Elizabeth became Queen most people lived in the countryside. They did not have to move to find work. Many spent all of their lives in the same village, never once leaving it.

They worked on land owned by rich farmers called yeomen. With their wages, farm workers could rent a cottage and some land. They could usually grow enough food for themselves, and their sheep provided them with wool to make clothes. There was never much left over to sell.

People had lived like this for hundreds of years, but times were changing. Some of the yeomen started to grow crops to sell in the towns. To make bigger profits they wanted more land. In many parts of England they took land which did not belong to them and fenced it in.

Often it was the common or waste land of a village. Here everyone had grazed their sheep and cattle. But not any more. Forests nearby had supplied the villagers with wood and acorns for their pigs. Soon the trees were cut down to make large fields with hedges planted around them. People noticed other changes too.

Yeomen began to charge higher rents for their land. Farmworkers who could not pay were forced to leave their homes and give back the land they had rented. To the yeomen, farming was a business. They wanted to make the best use of their fields.

This meant keeping sheep instead of growing corn. There was more money to be made by selling wool and some yeomen stopped growing corn altogether.

B *Threshing corn. Winnowing corn. A picture from medieval times.*

C *Sowing and harrowing the seed.*

D *Ploughing.*

E *A shepherd watches his flock.*

All the time farmworkers worried about losing their jobs. If they became ill or too old there were always other workers to replace them. This left their families without help of any kind.

They would then have no choice but to move to another village to find work, or start a new life in the towns. Many never made it. According to one writer they were allowed to lie by the roadside and die like animals.

F *This source describes what happened in Wormleighton, a village in Warwickshire, about 1560.*

William Coope took twelve houses with land attached, three cottages and 240 acres of **arable** land. These used to be ploughed annually to grow corn. He enclosed the land with hedges and ditches on all sides and let the houses and cottages fall into decay and ruin. He changed the arable land into pasture for animals. Sixty people who lived here and cultivated the land were forced tearfully to leave. They wandered without work and presumably they died.

G *Estimated population growth in England, 1541–1601.*

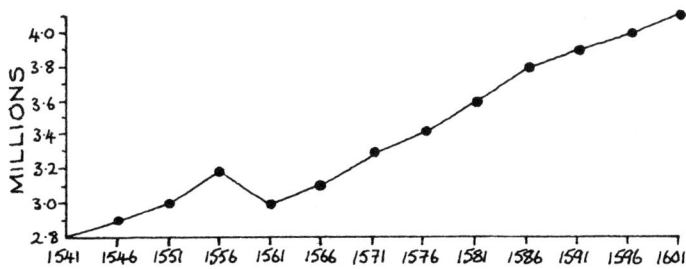

Activities

1. a) Sources A–D show jobs involved in growing corn. List the sources in the order that you think the jobs were done.
   b) Next to each source write a sentence to describe what you think is happening.

2. Look closely at source E. Explain why people shown in the other sources might not be pleased about the change from growing corn to sheep farming.

3. a) Read source F. What was the land around Wormleighton used for before 1560, and after it?
   b) Do you think this writer agrees or disagrees with what William Coope did? Explain your answer.

4. a) Look at the graph. What was the increase in population between 1561 and 1601?
   b) What effect do you think this would have on the price of corn? Give reasons.

8 A Farm Worker's Life

A *A 16th-century farmyard scene.*

In Elizabethan times, just like today, the work done on a farm depended on which season it was. During December and January, little could be done in the fields because the ground was often frozen. But wood still had to be cut and hedges repaired.

Ploughing usually took place in spring when wheat and barley were sown. Throughout the winter, any cattle had been chained up. Now they could be turned out onto the meadows to feed on the spring grass.

Spring was also the lambing season. Yeomen farmers might have to work late at night, but the hours of all their workers were fixed by law. Between March and September they started at 5am and did not finish until 7 or 8pm. During the rest of the year they worked from dawn till dusk.

Farm workers had a two-hour dinner break with thirty minutes extra between May and September. This was the busiest time of the farming year. Sheep had to be washed and sheared and there was more ploughing to be done. Women and children helped by weeding and picking stones from the fields.

Then came haymaking. Every patch of ground was cut to provide the cattle with winter fodder. August and September was harvest time. The corn was cut and later there were apples and berries to be picked.

In November, the pigs were slaughtered and as much meat as possible was salted or smoked in the farmhouse chimney. It was important too to store enough firewood and repair any buildings before the winter storms.

William Robinson was a farm worker. He lived at Upton, a small village in Nottinghamshire, until his death in 1600.

B *This is an **inventory**. It gives the value of William Robinson's possessions at the time of his death. (12d = 1s and 20s = £1)*

His money and clothes	20s

In the Living Room

2 brass pots, 2 small pans, a **cauldron**	18s
8 **pewter** dishes, 3 salt cellars, 3 candlesticks	7s
A cupboard	6s 8d
A table, a form, a plank, a chair, 2 stools, a milk churn, 6 bowls, 2 barrels	2s 8d
A poker, a **spit**, iron **reckons** attached to a **gallow balke**	2s

In the Parlour

2 cows and a **heifer**	£4 3s 4d
A young pig	3s
A cockerel and 2 hens	12d

In the Chamber (Upstairs)

A bed, a wash tub and **warming pan**	3s
A covering for a feather mattress, 6 pillows and 5 blankets	17s
5 pillow cases, 2 napkins	6s 8d
4 chests	5s
Painted wall coverings in the house and chamber, ladders and all other wood in or about the yard	3s 4d
Total	£8 18s 8d

At first glance you might think that this source is not very useful. But, by careful questioning it can tell us a lot about his life and the lives of other farm workers in Elizabethan times.

C *This modern picture shows what William Robinson's house might have looked like inside.*

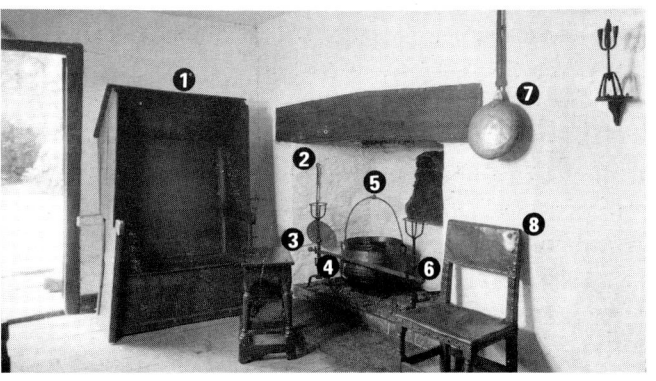

D *This 17th century source describes the kind of work that William Robinson would have done.*

The ploughman rises before 4am and first, feeds his cattle and cleans the cowshed. Then he makes his horses and the stable as clean as can be. He gives water to his cattle and horses, and food — dry peas or oats.

While they are eating, the ploughman gets ready his collars, harnesses and plough gear. This takes from 4am to 6am. After his breakfast he has half an hour to harness his cattle and at 7am he starts work. He ploughs until two and three in the afternoon.

Then he unfastens his cattle and brings them home, having cleansed them of dirt and filth. He feeds them and has his dinner about 4pm. After this he goes to his cattle again, cleans their stalls and gives them more food. Then he goes to the barn to get cattle food ready for the next day.

By this time it is about 6pm, and time for his supper. After supper he either sits by the fireside, mends shoes for himself or the family, or stamps apples for cider. He does this until 8pm. Then he takes his lantern and sees that his cattle are safely tied. And, after praying to God, he and his family go to sleep.

Activities

1. a) Read source B. How many rooms were there in William's house?
   b) What were they used for?
   c) Do you think William lived alone, or with his family? Give reasons for your answer.
   d) What were William's most valuable possessions?
   e) Write down five ways in which your home is different to William Robinson's.

2. Look at source C. Make a list, 1–8 and write down the name of each numbered object. Use source B to help you.

3. Study source A and make up four questions about it. Then ask a friend to try to answer them.

4. Read source D. Use this and any of the other sources to write or tape an imaginary television interview with William Robinson about his life.

9 Growing Up in Elizabethan Times

A *This painting shows an Elizabethan family in 1567.*

In Elizabethan times, children got up as soon as it was light. They washed in a bowl of water, fetched from a stream or well nearby, then got dressed. They wore the same style of clothes as their parents. This reminded children that they were expected to behave like adults.

For breakfast there would be coarse brown bread made of oats or barley. White bread made from wheat was expensive and only rich families could afford it. There was no tea or coffee. Children drank either milk or **ale**.

School started at 7am and was for boys aged 7 to 13. Their teachers were not trained and parents had to find the most suitable person they could. In country areas the local priest might teach boys in a room in the church.

Rich families paid for their sons to go to grammar schools. The main subjects were Greek, Latin and English, but sometimes there were lessons in history and drawing too. Discipline was strict. Often boys were beaten with a stick for answering a question wrongly. Prayers were said three times a day.

Lunch time was usually between 12 and 1pm. Afternoon lessons went on until 6pm with only a 15-minute break in the middle. There were fewer school holidays. Christmas was the longest with 16 days, but there were no half-term holidays.

Girls were usually taught at home by their mothers. They might learn to read and write. But most of their time was spent learning how to cook and mend clothes.

Children with poor parents were sometimes brought up by a foster mother, paid for by the church. She would teach them a trade. Girls learnt to spin and weave wool into cloth, boys learnt woodwork.

At 13 many boys started work. They might help their fathers with farm work or train as an apprentice to a tradesman, perhaps a carpenter or baker. The training was for seven years and in that time the boy would live in the tradesman's house.

Nobles and lords also sent their sons away from home. They went to live in the houses of other nobles to learn good manners.

After the evening meal there was usually time for children to play. Bedtime depended on the time of year. In winter, with only light from the fire and a few candles, most families were in bed by 9pm.

B *This account describes young people's rights in the 17th century.*

1. At 14, a son can choose his guardian, agree to marriage and make a will.
2. At 15, he has to swear **allegiance** to the King.
3. At 21, he is said to be fully grown up and can make any **contracts**.
4. At 7, a daughter can agree to marry, though afterwards she may change her mind.
5. At 12, if she has not changed her mind, she will be married for ever. Then she can make a will of her possessions.
6. At 16, she can live with her husband.

On a father's death, the eldest son inherits all the lands, the younger children receive the other possessions. If there is no son, the lands as well as the possessions are equally divided amongst the daughters.

C *A classroom scene in Elizabethan times.*

D *The first thing that children learned to write was their name, copied from an alphabet like this.*

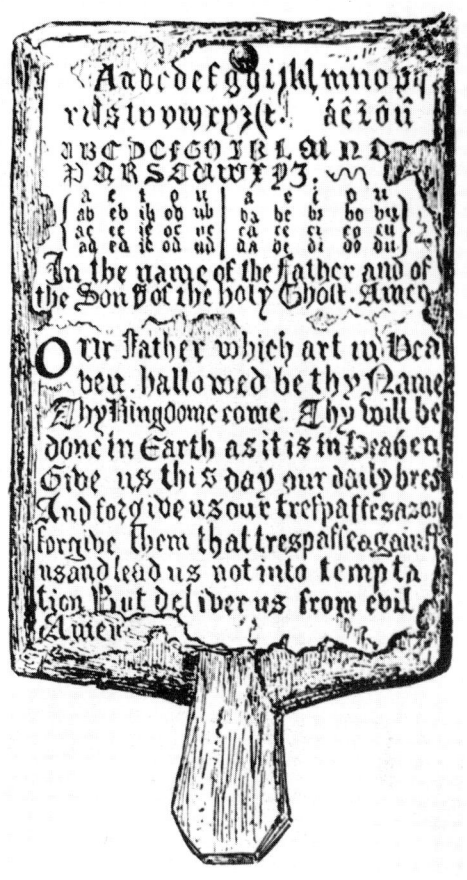

Activities

1. Read this chapter again. Make a list of the differences in children's lives today compared with Elizabethan times.

2. a) Look at source A. Do you think this family was rich or poor? Give reasons.
   b) Does this source prove that Elizabethan children always dressed like their parents? Explain your answer.

3. a) Describe what is happening in Source C.
   b) Do you think it was right to treat boys in this way? Give reasons.

4. a) Read source B. In what ways were girls treated differently from boys?
   b) Does this source suggest that girls were more, or less, important than boys? Explain your answer.

23

10 Captain John Hawkins: Trader or Pirate?

A *A 16th-century picture of Captain John Hawkins.*

Years before Elizabeth became Queen, Spanish and Portuguese explorers had travelled away from Europe to other lands. Soon, Spanish settlers were living in Central and South America. At the same time, the Portuguese built new settlements in Africa and India.

Portuguese settlers sent cotton, spices and silk back to their country. In *their* lands the Spanish had discovered gold and silver and were sending it to Spain by the shipload.

People made a fortune from this trade. Because of this the settlers were not allowed to do business with merchants from other countries. There were severe punishments for anyone who was caught doing so.

In the West Indies, Spanish settlers traded in secret with Captain John Hawkins. He was an English merchant. He bought slaves in Africa and sold them to the Spanish at a profit. The settlers wanted slaves to work in their sugar plantations.

In 1569 Captain Hawkins made his third voyage to the West Indies. He had ten ships and 500 slaves on board. In June he sailed to the port of Rio de la Hacha.

So far he had sold slaves in all the ports he had been to, and from the settlers he had bought food and supplies whenever he wanted them. This time it was different.

The next two sources explain what happened.

B *The Spanish treasurer wrote this account in a letter to the King on 26 September 1568.*

On June 10, John Hawkins, the English pirate, arrived off this port with ten warships. He had more than 600 men armed with weapons suitable for an attack. Their ships had many guns. For this reason, Miguel de Castellanas, the King's general in command, was unable to prevent them from landing.

He went out to meet them with 60 men. With this small force, he offered as fine and brave a defence as has ever been made in this land. He killed more than 30 of the enemy. Everyone was astonished at his great courage. He withdrew with this small force without losing a man, and the English general took the town. He burned two-thirds of it and blew up the government house.

Next day he began to march inland. Observing this, the King's general took his men to a position ahead of him to prevent his advance. Because of this, the English general decided to return to the town. He intended to march inland again at night.

Three hours before dawn they arrived at the place where the King's general had a tent. Nearby were the citizens of the town with all their possessions. The enemy captured a married man with his wife and children and other citizens. The Englishman told them that he would kill them and steal everything they had.

The King's general was very sorry for these people and he decided to pay a ransom — 4,000 pesos in gold. When he received the ransom the Englishman landed 75 slaves in the town. He did this, rather than throw them overboard, because they were dying on his hands. They were old men and young children, and among them all there wasn't a slave worth anything. He said he left them in payment for the damage he had done.

C *Captain Hawkins wrote this account in 1568.*

The treasurer, who was in charge of this town would not agree to any trade, or let us have any water. He had reinforced his town and built walls in all the places where it could be entered. He had 100 soldiers. He thought he would starve us and force us to land our slaves.

We had to get into the town and so with 200 men we broke down the walls. We entered the town with the loss of only one or two men on our side. No harm was done to the Spaniards, because after they fired their first volley of shots, they all ran away.

Then, because the Spanish wanted our slaves, and because of the friendship of the treasurer, we started a secret trade. The Spaniards came at night and bought 200 from us. In all the other places where we traded, the Spanish people welcomed us and traded willingly.

D *John Hawkins and his men enter Rio de la Hacha as drawn by a modern artist.*

E *After 1570 English ships regularly attacked Spanish towns in the West Indies. This 16th-century picture shows a raid by Sir Francis Drake.*

Activities

1 a) Read sources B and C. Divide a half page in your notebook into two columns headed B and C. Then, answering the questions below, fill in the differences between the two sources.
   Why did English ships come to the port?
   How many Spanish soldiers were there?
   How many English soldiers attacked?
   How many English soldiers were killed?
   How many Spanish soldiers were killed?
   What damage was caused to the town?
   How many slaves were landed?
   b) Why do you think the two accounts are different?
   c) In his letter to the King, what reasons would the Spanish treasurer have had to make up some of the things that happened?
   d) Would Captain Hawkins have any reason to make up some of the things that happened? Give reasons.
   e) Write your own account of what happened using only facts that the Spanish Ambassador and Captain Hawkins agree upon.

2 a) Look at source E and describe what you think is happening.
   b) Would this picture make English seamen want to sail with Sir Francis Drake or not? Explain why you think this.

25

11 Women in Elizabethan Times

A *A 17th-century ducking-stool.*

B *Four Elizabethan women.*

'I know I have the body of a weak and feeble woman.' These are supposed to be the words of Elizabeth I. She was Queen of England and more powerful than any man. But her views on women were clear.

Most people in England agreed with her: women were not equal to men. They were weaker and less intelligent. Because of this, women were expected to have just two ambitions — to get married and become an obedient wife. Then they would have a husband to protect them — someone to make all the important decisions.

Even their choice of husband was not theirs alone. Before a girl could marry she had to have her father's consent. If he did not approve, she had to find someone else.

They were encouraged to have large families. Women who gave birth to ten or more children were not unusual. By having this number of children there was a chance that some at least would survive. Sickness or disease killed the rest.

Large families also meant there were more children to help with the work. Boys went with their fathers to work in the fields. Girls worked in the house. They helped their mothers to cook, make clothes and nurse any smaller children.

A farmer's wife would milk the cows and make her own butter and cheese. This, and any vegetables they had grown, she could sell at the local market and keep any profit for herself.

In Elizabethan times make-up was used by men and women. It was not fashionable to have sun-tanned skin, so people whitened their face with white lead. This, and the **belladonna** they used to line their eyes, was poisonous. So too was the mercury which was used to treat a bad complexion.

It helps to explain why so many men and women died before they were middle-aged. They slowly poisoned themselves to death.

C *In 1600 William Vaughn described some of the duties of husbands and wives.*

1. He must patiently put up with the harshness of his wife, because there is nothing in the world more spiteful than a woman who is annoyed.
2. The husband must not injure his wife by word or deed, for a woman is a feeble creature. She does not have as much noble courage as a man.
3. The husband must provide for his wife and for her housekeeping according to his ability.
4. The husband must make sure his wife is happy with him, otherwise she will find some place to gossip in.

But what shall the woman do? Shall she do what seems good in her own eyes? No; for St. Peter speaks to wives like this: 'Let wives be subject to their husbands.'

1. She must not dress too finely because frizzled hair, embroidery, precious stones and gaudy clothes can lead to adultery.
2. She must not be jealous or mistrust her husband if he is away.
3. The wife must carefully look after the household and bring up her children and servants to fear God.

D *Wash day in 1582.*

E *This 16th-century account is quoted in* How they Lived, *edited by M. Harrison and O. M. Royston in 1963.*

In this country **proceedings** aren't carried on by people's sworn spoken or written evidence. They are carried on by the opinion of men. It is the easiest thing in the world to get a person thrown into prison in this country. For every officer of justice has the power of arresting any one at the request of a private individual. Nor is there any punishment for a **slanderous** accusation.

F *This account is taken from the court records of Avely Manor (1592).*

The wife of Walter Hycocks and the wife of Peter Philips are common **scolds**. Therefore it is ordered that they shall be told in church to stop their scolding. But if their neighbours complain a second time, they shall be punished by the ducking stool.

Activities

1. a) Describe what you think is happening in source A.
   b) Does this source prove that women were badly treated in Elizabethan times? Explain your answer.

2. Read source E and source F. Do you think it is likely that the women in source F were given a fair trial? Give reasons.

3. a) Read source C. List three words or phrases which show whether this writer had a good opinion, or a bad opinion of women.
   b) According to this writer, what are the main jobs of a woman?
   c) Make a list of what you think are the main duties of husbands and wives today.
   d) How are they different from source C?

4. Look at source B. Which woman is probably the poorest? Explain how you decided.

5. Most of our evidence about women in Elizabethan times was produced by men. Why is it important to remember this as you read this chapter?

12 Mary, Queen of Scots

A *This picture of Mary's execution was painted in the 19th century.*

Mary, Queen of Scots, had been a prisoner in England since 1568. She had her own servants, friends were allowed to stay with her and she could go hunting whenever she liked. Elizabeth, who was her cousin, wanted her to be well looked after.

Meanwhile, in secret, Mary read letters from Catholics in England and Spain. They were full of plans to set her free. The Spanish army would invade. Or Elizabeth would be murdered — blown up by gunpowder, or poisoned in her sleep. All these plans ended with Mary as the new Catholic Queen of England.

Mary got involved in three of these plans. Each time she was found out. The fourth, in 1586, cost her her life. It was the idea of Sir Francis Walsingham, Elizabeth's Chief Secretary. He had thought of a way to trap Mary once and for all.

In 1585 she was moved to Chartley Castle. Few people were allowed in or out. Mary was closely watched and all of her letters were read.

The Chief Secretary ordered one of his spies to visit Mary's Catholic friends. He told them that there was a way of getting messages to and from Mary smuggled in barrels of beer. Soon the letters started to arrive.

Once again they contained plans to free Mary and kill Elizabeth. The Chief Secretary read the letters, put them back in the barrels and waited for Mary to reply.

When she did so, he copied her letter, then sent it out. But only after forging part of it himself. This letter was used as evidence against Mary.

Anthony Babington and eleven other Catholics involved in the plan were hung, drawn and quartered. Their remains were stuck on to London's city gates. At her trial, Mary was found guilty and condemned to death. People waited for the Queen to order her death warrant . . . but for months she refused to do it.

B *Mary's execution painted in 1587.*

Elizabeth even hinted to Mary's jailers that they could kill her in secret. It would save Elizabeth from taking the blame for her death.

These sources explain what happened next.

C *William Camden wrote this account in 1615. It is from a book he wrote in praise of Queen Elizabeth.*

The Queen spent all her time alone, sad and often sighing to herself. In the middle of her confused thoughts she gave a letter to Davison, one of her secretaries. She ordered a warrant to be drawn up for Mary's execution and told him not to tell anyone. But the next day she changed her mind and told Davison not to draw up the warrant. Davison came to the Queen and told her that he had already done it. She was angry at this and blamed him for being hasty.

In spite of this, Davison told her Council of Ministers about the warrant. He easily persuaded them that the Queen had ordered the execution to be carried out. Without any delay Beale was sent down with one or two executioners and a warrant. This ordered the Earl of Shrewsbury and others to see that the execution was carried out. This was without any knowledge of the Queen at all. At this very moment she told Davison that she would take another course with the Queen of Scots. But for all this, he did not call Beale back.

D *Robert Wyngfeld was present at Mary's execution. He wrote this account a few days after her death.*

Without any terror of the place, she came into the hall and stepped up to the scaffold. A stool was brought to her. She sat down and began to pray very quickly in Latin. In the middle of her prayers she cried so much that she slipped off her stool.

Then the two executioners kneeled down and asked her to forgive them. She answered, 'I forgive you with all my heart.' Then with the help of her two women, she began to undress.

During this she smiled and said that she had never taken off her clothes before such a crowd of people. When she had undressed to her petticoat, the two women burst into pitiful shrieking and crying. The Queen made the sign of the cross over them, said goodbye to them and prayed.

Then she laid herself upon the block most quietly and stretched out her arms and legs. At last while one of the executioners held her straightly with one of his hands, the other gave two strokes of an axe before he cut off her head.

E *Queen Elizabeth wrote this to Mary's son, James VI of Scotland on 14 February 1587.*

I wish you knew the extreme sadness that overwhelms me because of this sad accident. It has happened against my wishes. God and many others know how innocent I am in this matter. I know she has deserved this, but if I had meant it to happen, I would not have got others to do it. I will never accuse myself with something that I had not even thought of.

F *Mary, Queen of Scots' death mask.*

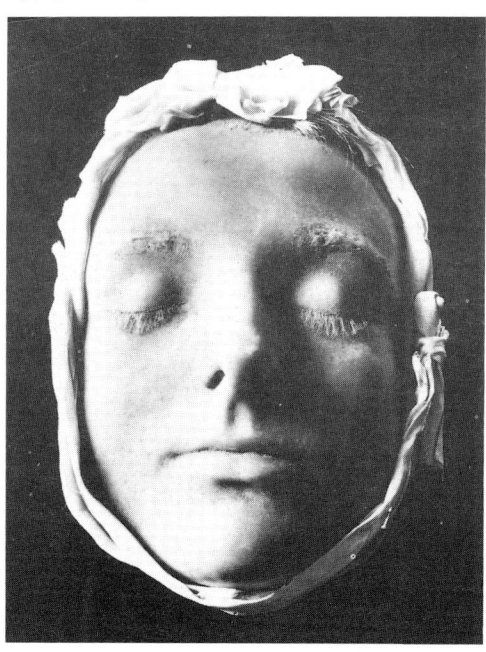

Activities

1   a) Read source C. Do you think this source gives a good impression of Queen Elizabeth or not? Explain your answer.
    b) Why might this source not give the whole truth about Elizabeth's involvement in Mary's execution?

2   What impression do you get of Elizabeth from source E?

3   a) Read source D and select from this list three words which you think best describe Mary: weak, religious, sad, strong, tearful, brave, calm, terrified, cheerful, cowardly, kind.
    b) Next to each word write out a sentence from the source that you think shows this.

4   a) List three facts about the execution described in source D but not shown in source A.
    b) Source A was painted in the 19th century. Does this mean that it is bound to be less reliable than source B? Explain your answer.

13 The Spanish Armada, 1588

For King Philip II it was the final insult. That morning, 20 April 1587, Sir Francis Drake had attacked Cadiz harbour and sunk 24 Spanish ships.

He wanted revenge and ordered a huge fleet to be built — the Armada. With it, King Philip planned to invade England and get rid of Elizabeth once and for all.

He was already angry with her for sending an army to the Netherlands. Here her soldiers

A *Ships of the Spanish Armada.*

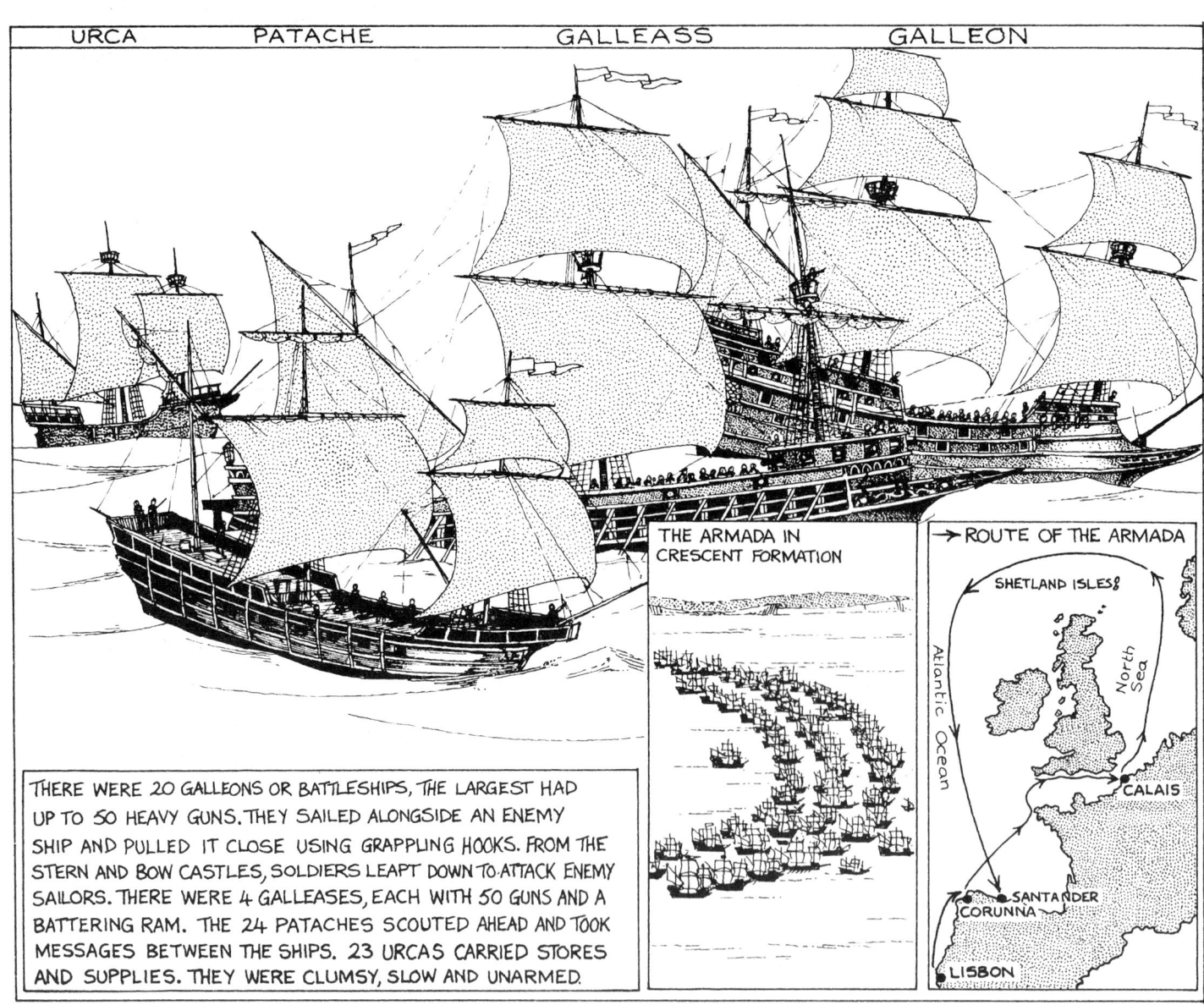

THERE WERE 20 GALLEONS OR BATTLESHIPS, THE LARGEST HAD UP TO 50 HEAVY GUNS. THEY SAILED ALONGSIDE AN ENEMY SHIP AND PULLED IT CLOSE USING GRAPPLING HOOKS. FROM THE STERN AND BOW CASTLES, SOLDIERS LEAPT DOWN TO ATTACK ENEMY SAILORS. THERE WERE 4 GALLEASES, EACH WITH 50 GUNS AND A BATTERING RAM. THE 24 PATACHES SCOUTED AHEAD AND TOOK MESSAGES BETWEEN THE SHIPS. 23 URCAS CARRIED STORES AND SUPPLIES. THEY WERE CLUMSY, SLOW AND UNARMED.

fought alongside Protestants who had rebelled against King Philip. He complained too about English pirates — sea captains who attacked and looted Spanish treasure ships.

But Elizabeth also had reason to be angry. Three times, Catholics in England had plotted to kill her. Each time the Spanish King had been involved.

Years before, King Philip had proposed marriage to Elizabeth. Now they prepared for war.

According to King Philip's plan, the Armada would take 19,000 soldiers from Spain to the Netherlands. Here it would meet up with another Spanish army already in position. Then, this combined force of 35,000 men would sail across the English Channel and march quickly to London.

Along the south coast of England people waited. Then, on 29 July came the news. The Armada had been spotted five miles out to sea. The English fleet of about 100 ships waited until it passed Plymouth.

Each fleet had roughly the same number of galleons. But while the Spanish ships were tall and heavy — a larger target to hit — English galleons were low and slim. They were faster too and could turn more easily.

The Armada crept slowly along the coast in a tight **crescent** formation. For the English ships sailing behind, this made it difficult to attack. They could not get in amongst the Spanish fleet to fire their guns **broadside**. The risk of being boarded by Spanish soldiers was too great.

B *This is an extract from a letter written by King Philip to the Duke of Medina Sidonia, the Commander of the Armada.*

> You must remember that the enemy's object will be to fight at long range because of his advantage in **artillery**. So the aim of our men must be to bring him to close quarters and grapple with him. The enemy uses his artillery in order to deliver his fire low and sink his opponents' ships. You will take what precautions you think necessary.

C *This extract is taken from* The Armada *by John Hale (1913).*

> In the major English ships, gun drill was fairly well organised and men could load their guns and fire them quickly — the Spaniards said three times as fast as they could do it themselves.

D *This 19th-century engraving shows a scene on board the English ship,* Ark Royal.

E *The Duke of Medina Sidonia wrote this in his diary in August 1588.*

> Our ships are too heavy, compared with the lightness of the enemy's.

Activities

1. a) Copy the picture of the Armada's crescent formation into your book.
    b) Draw arrows on your picture to show where you would put these ships in the Armada's formation: carracks, pataches, urcas, galleons, galleasses.
    c) Underneath write a short paragraph to explain how you decided where to position these ships.
    d) Why was the crescent formation difficult to attack?

2. a) Read source B. Use this source and information in the chapter to describe the Armada's fighting tactics.
    b) Read source C and source E. Use these sources and information in this chapter to explain why it was difficult for Spanish ships to follow these tactics.

3. Look at source D. Describe as fully as possible what you think is happening.

The Armada is defeated

A A Spanish captain surrenders to Sir Francis Drake in this 19th-century painting.

On 6 August the Armada dropped anchor off Calais. Waiting only 20 miles inland was the second Spanish army. The English fleet had to stop them meeting. But so far, its ships had fired from too far away to do any real damage.

Then came the fire ships — eight of them, filled by the English with anything that would burn. That night, as the wind blew harder, they set them ablaze and sent them straight at the Armada.

In panic, the Spanish ships tried to escape. Their sailors cut anchors in their hurry to get away. Slower ships drifted into the darkness . . . and danger.

Not one ship was destroyed by fire. But next morning it was clear that the Armada's crescent formation had been broken.

Immediately the English attacked, much closer than before. Spanish ships were shot through with holes, and flying splinters caused terrible injuries to the sailors on board. Then the gales began.

High winds whipped up the sea and the English fleet turned back to port. For the Spanish this was not possible. They had to weather the storm as waves crashed over their leaking ships.

The gales blew the Armada into the North Sea, miles off course. The invasion plan had failed. All that remained was to get back to Spain as quickly as possible. But this meant sailing with the wind around Scotland and Ireland, in some of the most dangerous seas in the world.

Supplies of food and water were very low. There was none to spare for the hundreds of horses on board so they were thrown into the sea. Gradually men became too weak to do repairs and keep the pumps going.

Ships filled with water, sank lower in the waves and then disappeared. Others were wrecked off the Irish coast.

Out of the Armada's 130 ships, only 60 returned. No one knows for certain how many men died — perhaps 19,000. On some ships men died of starvation or thirst within sight of Spain.

The Armada had failed. For the time being, England was safe.

B *This is an extract from a poem written by Queen Elizabeth in 1588.*

He made the winds and waters rise to scatter all mine enemies.

C *Armada ships had to be repaired on the voyage back to Spain. A modern artist's impression.*

D *This account is quoted in* The Voyage of the Armada *by David Howarth (1981). It is based on a letter written by Captain Francisco de Cuellar to a friend in October 1589.*

Captain de Cuellar's ship ran aground in a gale off a sandy beach called Streedagh Sound on the west coast of Ireland. Within an hour his ship was smashed to bits. Cuellar could not swim. He held on till the last possible moment while men were swept overboard.

'The waves and the storm were very great. On the other hand, the land and shore were full of enemies. They ran about jumping and dancing with joy at our misfortune. When one of our people reached the beach, 200 savages stripped him naked.'

Cuellar saw a hatch cover floating and got onto it. Unfortunately another piece of timber crushed his legs. Then he was thrown ashore. 'The enemies on the beach did not approach me, seeing me with legs and hands covered with blood. I crawled on, little by little. I stopped for the night in a deserted place and lay down in great pain on some rushes.'

By the next morning English soldiers had arrived. Cuellar dragged himself away to an abbey where he found twelve Spaniards hanging from the rafters. In the woods he met two Irishmen who stripped him of his remaining clothes, and an Englishman who attacked him with a knife. He was saved by a very beautiful girl but she stole his **reliquary**. It was all he had left.

He stumbled into the nearest village. Here somebody gave him a blanket full of bugs and he wandered off again. On the road he met a priest who directed him to a castle 20 miles away. Before he found it, he met a blacksmith who tricked him into his hut, then forced him to work. But the priest turned up again, rescued him and took him to the castle.

E *In his book,* The Armada *(1913), John Hale described how Captain Francisco de Cuellar escaped from Ireland.*

Cuellar helped the O'Rourke clan defend their castle against the English. Then he made his way northwards. It was to a Catholic bishop that he owed his final escape. Although he was very poor, the bishop had helped a number of shipwrecked Spaniards. With some of these, Cuellar sailed in a boat to Scotland — and from there to the Spanish army in Flanders.

Activities

1 In source A, which man do you think is Sir Francis Drake? Give reasons.

2 a) Read source D and source E. What evidence might help you to check whether this story was true or not?
   b) Design a cover for a book about Captain de Cuellar's escape.
   c) Write a 100-word summary of the book to make people want to read it.

3 Look at source C and describe what repairs are being done.

4 a) According to source B, how was the Armada beaten?
   b) From all the information in this chapter, do you agree or disagree with this verdict?

5 In England medals were made after the Armada with these words, 'God breathed and they were scattered.' Include these words in your own design for an Armada medal.

14 Sport and Entertainment

For most people in Elizabethan times, Sunday was their day off. After church service in the morning there were many games and sports they could play. Football was one of their favourites, but it was very different to the game played today.

A *Cock-fighting was a popular sport.*

B *Bear baiting.*

There was no pitch, no limit to the number in each team and no rules. At each end of the village was a goal — perhaps a tree or someone's house. A pig's bladder would do for the ball. And this could be thrown, kicked, or carried by anyone who wanted to join in.

Hundreds often did. But in the fighting and wrestling that took place, people risked being seriously injured or even killed.

Cock throwing and dog tossing were two other popular sports. In the first, a cock was tied to a post and then pelted with sticks. People betted on how long the cock would survive.

In the second, a dog was put in a blanket and tossed into the air. People took bets on how many times the dog could be tossed before it fell out.

There was even more gambling on cock-fights. In this sport, birds ripped each other to pieces with their beaks and with razor-sharp spurs strapped to their legs.

Usually it was a fight between just two birds; but sometimes twenty or more were thrown into the cock-pit and allowed to fight until only one was left. All the time, the spectators took bets on which bird would win.

In many villages and towns bull rings were built. Here people watched as bulls, bears and even horses were tied to a stake and attacked by large dogs.

In the surrounding woodlands, deer were hunted with hounds or shot with crossbows. Hunting with hawks and hare coursing were also popular. So too was fishing which was enjoyed by both men and women.

People enjoyed singing and dancing too, especially at Church Ales. These were parties given by the village priest. Afterwards people might watch a play performed in the yard of a local inn.

When it rained there were always indoor games to play: dice, draughts and merelles were some of the most popular.

C *A merelles board.*

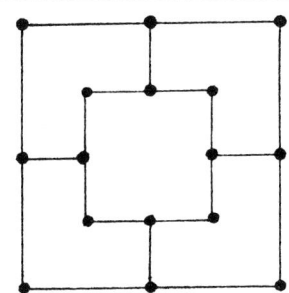

Two people can play merelles. Each player has five counters. They take it in turn to place counters one at a time on the dots. The object is to get a row of three. Each player tries to block the other from doing this. If all the counters are on the board and neither player has got a row of three, the counters can be slid one at a time. The first player to get a row of three is the winner.

D *In 1599 Thomas Platter described what was involved in bull and bear baiting.*

Every Sunday and Wednesday in London there are bear baitings. The theatre is circular with galleries round the top for the spectators. The ground space down below is empty.

Here a large bear on a long rope was tied to a stake. Then a number of great English **mastiffs** were brought in and shown to the bear.

After this they baited the bear, one after another. Although the dogs were struck and mauled by the bear, they did not give in. They had to be pulled off by sheer force and the muzzles forced open with long sticks. The bear's teeth were not sharp so they could not injure the dogs; they have them broken short.

When the first mastiffs tired, fresh ones were brought in to bait the bear. When the bear was tired, a powerful white bull was then brought in. One dog at a time was set on him. He speared those with his horns and tossed them so they could not get the better of him. And as the dogs fell to the floor again, several men held sticks under them to break their fall. Lastly they brought in an old, blind bear which boys hit with canes and sticks. But he knew how to untie his lead, and he ran back to his stall.

E *This description of Church Ales was written by Philip Stubbes in 1585.*

The Church wardens, with the agreement of everyone in the parish, give 20 **quarts** of **malt**. Some of it is bought out of church funds, and some of it is given by the villagers themselves. This malt is made into very strong ale or beer and is sold in the church. The man who spends the most drinking it is counted the godliest because he is spending it on his church! In this way they continue for six weeks, swilling night and day until they are as drunk as rats and as stupid as cattle.

F *Church Ales were a popular part of village life — a modern artist's impression.*

Activities

1 List three differences between football played in Elizabethan times, and the game today.

2 a) According to source E how were churches able to raise money?
b) Do you think this writer approves of Church Ales or not?

3 a) What does source D tell you about people's attitudes to animals in Elizabethan times?
b) You own a theatre where bull and bear baiting take place. Design a poster to tell people when the next baiting will take place, or design a poster against it.

4 Design a merelles board in your book like the one above. Make ten counters and a board 10cm by 10cm, find a partner and you are ready to play merelles.

15 Dealing with the Poor

Every day in Elizabethan times, thousands of people went hungry. Their wages were so low that they could not buy enough food, or they were out of work and had no money at all. These were the poor people and there were more of them than ever before.

England's population was rising but in many parts of the country, the change to sheep farming meant there were fewer jobs. Those people who did have work found that prices went up faster than their wages.

There was no sick pay, no old age pension — none of the means by which people are helped today. If you were poor, you could beg for money, or steal it . . . or die of starvation. Some beggars were too old or too weak to work. Others did not want to. They were healthy and strong but found begging easier than work. They roamed the countryside, sometimes in groups of two or three, often in gangs of 40 or more. To get money they might pretend to be ill, deaf and dumb, or mad. Anyone who refused them risked being beaten up.

There were severe punishments for beggars like these. For a first offence they were whipped and burned through their right ear with a hot iron. If they were caught a second time, their left ear was burned through. The third time, they were hung.

People who were genuinely too ill to work did receive some help. Priests often gave out money from the church collection, or used money from the Church Ales, but it did not solve the problem.

So, in 1601 the Queen introduced a new tax: the Poor Rate. The old and sick were given a small pension from this. People who were young and healthy also got money, but they had to work for it. They were given wool, leather or iron to make things which could be sold.

A *Beggars were often severely treated.*

B *A beggar asking for help from a rich man.*

Each parish had to look after its own poor people. Anyone found without money or work was sent back to the place where they were born. But, as before, strangers who were caught begging were whipped or hung.

The Poor Rate helped thousands of poor people. They were never well off but now, at least, they did not have to starve to death.

C *In 1608 Thomas Dekker described how a rogue would beg for money.*

A rogue speaks in a sad voice and crawls along the street. He supports his body with a stick, as if there wasn't enough strength in his legs. His head is wrapped in cloth, and it is as filthy as his face. Their clothes are all tattered and often they have no shirt. But if they had better clothes given to them, they would only sell them to some of their friends. They wander up and down in this sad way just to make people feel sorry for them. At night they merrily spend the money they get.

D *This account of women beggars is quoted in* Tudor Economic Documents, *edited by R. H. Tawney and E. Power, 1951. (12d = 5p)*

Bawdy baskets are women who carry baskets on their arms. In these baskets they have lace, pins, needles and round, silk **girdles** of all colours. They buy rabbit skins and steal linen clothes off hedges. These they sell to maiden servants when their mistress is out of the way, for a good piece of bacon or beef. This might be worth 12d, but the things that they sell are worth only 2d.

E *People who could not pay their debts might be put in prison.*

F *A beggar's family.*

Activities

1 Why did the number of poor people increase in Elizabethan times?

2 a) Look at source A and explain what is happening.
b) Do you think it was fair to treat beggars in this way or not? Give reasons.
c) Why do you think beggars were whipped in front of other townspeople?

3 a) Read source C. What impression do you get of rogues from this source?
b) What advice do you think this writer would give to poor people in Elizabethan times?
c) Do you think this would be good advice or not? Explain your answer.

4 a) Read source D. Why might people leave linen clothes on hedges?
b) Does this source give a good or bad impression of servants? Give reasons.

5 a) Look at source B. What evidence is there that the beggar was poor?
b) Do you think that this woodcut was meant to criticise rich people or poor people? Give reasons for your answer.

6 a) Look at source F. Why might people who saw this beggar feel sorry for him?
b) Look closely at the woman. Do you think the artist feels sorry for beggars or not? Explain why you think this.

16 Virginia, England's First Colony

It was in Elizabethan times that people first left England to settle in America. For years, English boats had fished off America's eastern coast. But until now, no one had wanted to live there.

People changed their minds when they heard stories about gold and diamonds that could be found, and miles of good farmland which did not seem to belong to anyone. They wondered if the stories were true.

In 1584 two small ships set sail from Plymouth to find out. On board were 100 men led by Captain Phillip Amadas. They had enough food and supplies for six months and orders to take over any land that they found. Six weeks later they reached the coast of America, and dropped anchor next to a large island.

Queen Elizabeth had already chosen a name for this area: Virginia. The Indians who lived there called it Roanoke. After 1584 it belonged to England.

Captain Amadas and his men sailed back to England, pleased with what they had seen. With them they took two Indian warriors. Next year three more ships set out, again with 100 men. This time they had orders to stay.

On the island these men built a settlement of a few huts surrounded by a ditch and a wooden fence. This was the start of Britain's first **colony** in America.

There were plans for many more. With their safe harbours the colonies could provide a base for England's fighting ships. They would make it easier for them to attack the Spanish treasure fleet.

A *John White was one of the first settlers in Roanoke. He drew this picture to show the stages that went into making an Indian canoe. The different stages are numbered in order.*

38

Some people thought that colonies might help to solve England's unemployment problem. Those without work could be shipped to America. It would be better than having them begging and stealing in England.

All that remained was to make the colony of Virginia a success.

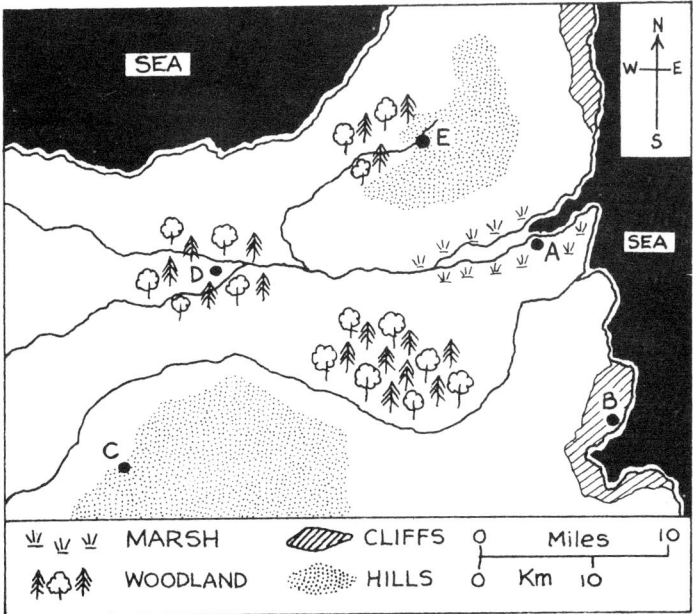

This map shows sites for a possible settlement in America

B *An eyewitness account of the first voyage to Virginia written by Captain Arthur Barlow in 1584.*

We had stayed by the side of the island for two days without seeing anyone. The third day we saw a small boat rowing towards us. This boat came to the beach some distance from our ships. There were three people in it. Two of them stayed in the boat. The third walked along the shore towards us.

We stayed on board and watched him walk up and down the beach next to us. Then Captain Amadas, myself and others rowed to the beach. This fellow watched us coming and didn't show any fear or doubt.

After he had spoken of many things that we could not understand, he agreed to come with us to our ships. Here we gave him a shirt and a hat. We made him taste our wine and our meat which he liked very much.

Then, after looking around our ships, he went to his own boat. He had left this in a small cove nearby. He started to fish, and in less than half an hour he had filled his boat with as many fish as it could carry.

He came again to the beach alongside us and there he divided his fish into two parts. He gave one part to our main ship, the other to our second ship. After this he went away.

C *Thomas Hariot sailed to Virginia and wrote this account of the Indians in 1588.*

Most things they saw, like compasses, magnets, telescopes, guns, hooks and clocks were very strange to them. They could not understand what they were or how they had come to be made. They thought they were the works of gods rather than men, or they had been given and taught us by the gods. This made them have a good opinion of us.

Activities

1 Imagine you are the leader of 100 settlers. Your ship is anchored at the mouth of a river, somewhere on the east coast of America. The map opposite shows five possible sites for a settlement.
   Alongside the rivers the land is suitable for growing crops and grazing cattle. You can cross any river up to ten miles from its mouth. Travel is by foot, or by river.
   a) Copy the map into your book.
   b) Write out a list like the one below. Fill in the good points and bad points for each site.

	Good	Bad
A		
B		
C		
D		
E		

   c) Choose the best site and mark it on your map. Explain how you chose it.
   d) Make a list of the things you would need for your settlement.

2 Look at source A. Describe the various stages that went into making an Indian canoe.

3 Read source B. You are the Indian who meets Captain Amadas and his men. Describe what happened to you, as well as your thoughts and feelings. Use source C to help you.

The colony fails

A *John White drew this picture of an Indian chief in 1585.*

At first the English settlers were accepted by the Indians. They stayed as their guests at Secoton, Virginia's main village. The Indians showed them trees and plants they had never seen before.

There was no gold to be found, but the warm climate made the settlers hope that spices, silk and sugar could be produced — and these were just as valuable.

The settlers described in their letters how different the Indian way of life was from their own. In spite of this they saw nothing to worry them. The Indians were friendly and they would not risk a fight because the settlers had far better weapons.

So it was a shock to people in England when the colony failed. The settlers could not grow enough food. Their supplies ran out, and they went home on the first English ship that reached them.

Two weeks later Captain Richard Grenville sailed to Virginia. He did not know that everyone had gone. So, when he saw the deserted settlement he left 15 men with two years' supplies. What happened to them then is a mystery.

In 1587 another 100 men and 17 women arrived at the settlement. They found that much of it had been destroyed. Nearby were the bones of one of the 15 men. There was no sign of the other 14.

We know this from the letters that these people wrote, but this is all the evidence they left. For they, like the 15 men before them, were never seen again.

This did not stop people from wanting to go to America, but it took another 40 years to set up an English colony that lasted.

B *This description of the Indians was written by Thomas Hariot in 1586.*

> They wear loose coverings made of deer skin and aprons made of the same material around their waists. Apart from this they are naked. They have no cutting tools, or weapons of iron and steel, and they don't know how to make any. Those weapons that they have are bows made of wood, and arrows made of reeds, and wooden truncheons. They defend themselves with armour made of sticks woven together with thread.
>
> If there are any wars between us and them, we have many advantages over them. This is because of our discipline and our strange weapons — especially our cannons. In our experience, their best defence was running away.
>
> In comparison to us they are a poor people because they do not have our skills and knowledge. But in their own way they are very clever. Although they have no tools or crafts, or sciences and arts like us, they show excellent intelligence in the things they do.
>
> When they consider by how much our knowledge and crafts are better than theirs, it is probable they will want our friendship and love. They will also have greater respect for pleasing and obeying us.

C *This picture of a hunting scene in Virginia was printed in 1619.*

D *Richard Hakluyt wrote this account in 1589.*

We shall not only receive many precious things from America. In time we will be able to sell hats, bonnets, knives, fish hooks, copper kettles, beads, looking glasses, bugles and thousands of other things. The people of that country will start to use them and make *our* country wonderfully rich.

E *The bodies of Indian chiefs were preserved in special houses.*

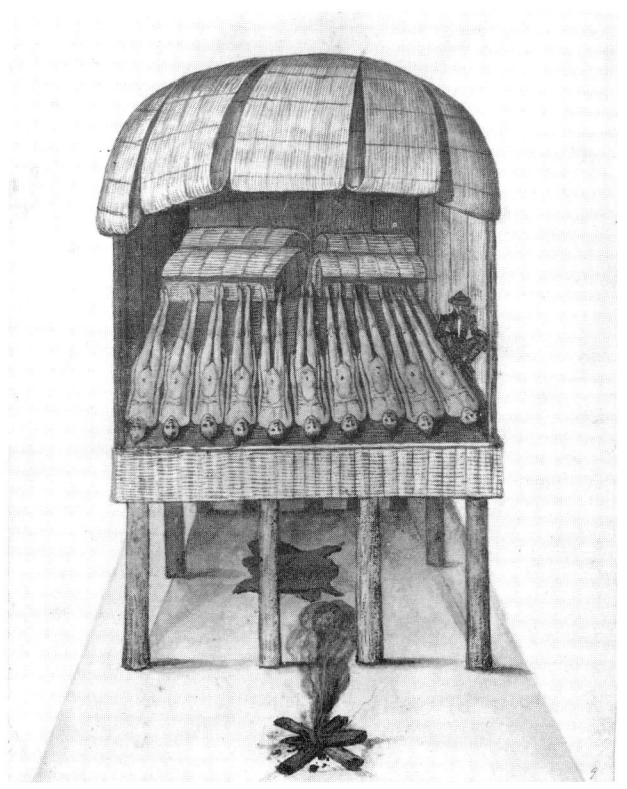

F *This 16th-century account describes one of the new plants found in America. It is quoted in* The Development of Natural History in Tudor England *(1969).*

You will see sailors and all others who come back from America using little funnels made of palm leaves or straw. At the end of these funnels they stuff the plant's crumbled dried leaves. This they light and opening their mouths as much as they can, they suck in the smoke with their breath. The sailors say this stops their hunger and thirst. It restores their strength and refreshes their spirits. This plant is a valuable remedy for sores, wounds, infections of the throat and chest and plague fever.

Activities

1. Describe the clothes of the Indian chief. Use source B to help you.

2. a) According to the writer of source B, why would the Indians not fight the English colonists?
   b) Does this writer think that the Indians are more intelligent than the English, less intelligent, or equal to them? Explain your answer.

3. a) Which plant do you think is being described in source F? Give reasons.
   b) What according to this writer are the benefits of this plant?
   c) Do doctors today agree with this writer's views? Explain your answer.

4. a) Look at source E. How were the bodies of Indian chiefs preserved?
   b) Why do you think they were preserved?

5. a) Look at source C. List the different types of hunting that you can see.
   b) Suppose you couldn't decide whether to become a settler in Virginia. Explain how this source might affect your decision.

6. Read source F. According to Richard Hakluyt, how would England benefit from having colonies in America?

17 Superstition and Witchcraft

A *A 17th-century print of three witches.*

In Elizabethan times nearly everybody believed in the supernatural. Many people would not go near a graveyard at night for fear of ghosts. They were **superstitious** and frightened of witches too.

It was bad luck if a hare crossed your path and worse still if you left empty egg shells lying about. Witches would use them as boats to travel around in.

Magic spells and lucky charms could keep away evil spirits. Some people thought they could stop sickness: one cure for a headache was to press a hangman's rope to your head.

In most villages and towns there was nearly always someone who could offer cures like these. Often they were old women who lived alone. Sometimes they helped as **midwives**, or sold magic cures made from herbs.

Usually there was some way that they were different to other people. They might behave strangely, have unusual birth marks or suffer from mental illness. Some people said these were signs that God had rejected them.

It was easy to blame them when things went wrong — if there was an outbreak of disease or if the harvest failed. People said they used their strange power to get revenge for being poor, lonely and different.

Women like these were sometimes accused of witchcraft. The accused woman would be tied up and thrown into a lake or river. If she floated, she was guilty. If the woman sank, then she was innocent.

B *This description of the devil was written by Reginald Scot in 1584.*

In our childhood, our mothers' maids terrified us with an ugly devil with horns on his head, fire in his mouth and a tail in his back, eyes like a basin, fangs like a dog, claws like a bear, a skin like a negro and a voice like a roaring lion.

...account is quoted in 'The Elizabethan ...issance,' by A. L. Rowse (1971).

...Throckmorton's girls started to have **fits** — it ...ay of drawing attention to themselves. They ...to dislike a poor neighbour, Mother Samuel, ...me to their house to work. They insisted they ...ewitched by her.

...en she kept away they had fits again and demanded that they must see her. Their uncles and some clergymen said that during their fits, the children made heavenly speeches to this old woman. These young children were obviously spoiled and would have been better for a good thrashing.

The poor woman began to believe that she was to blame for the fits. The children's uncle, Henry Pickering, told her that she should confess and beg forgiveness. If she did not do this, he said he hoped to see her burned at a stake.

Nothing happened to the children, but a few weeks later Mother Samuel had an argument with Lady Cromwell. She too had taken an interest in the girls. When she returned home, Lady Cromwell became ill. She began to have dreams about a witch and her cat. When she died, a year later, Mother Samuel was accused of causing her death.

At her trial, some of the **justices** were the girls' uncles. She was scratched by women and children to make the blood come out of her. Finally she was convinced that she was to blame for Lady Cromwell's death. This was equivalent to murder.

Her husband and daughter were accused of helping her. The daughter was made to repeat the words, 'I am a witch and agreed to the death of Lady Cromwell.' In April 1593 all three were hanged — mother, father and daughter.

D Witches hanged at Chelmsford in 1589.

E This picture shows a woman being tested to see if she is a witch.

Activities

1. Look at source A and the caption above it. Do you think, 'A 17th-century print of three women and their pets' would make a better caption or not? Explain your answer.

2. a) Read source C. How can you tell that the writer feels sorry for Mother Samuel?
   b) Do you think she had a fair trial or not? Give reasons for your answer.
   c) Where do you think the writer got his evidence from?

3. a) Read source B. Use the information in it to draw your own picture of the devil.
   b) Why do you think mothers' maids would make the devil sound so horrible?

18 The Essex Rebellion, 1601

Queen Elizabeth was growing old. One by one her most trusted advisors died. By 1598 Sir Francis Walsingham, Lord Burghley and the Earl of Leicester were all dead.

Thirty years before there had been rumours that Elizabeth and the Earl were lovers. They had stayed friends and in a box by her bedside, Elizabeth kept the last letter he wrote to her.

After his death she spent much of her time with his stepson, Robert Devereux, Earl of Essex. He was a national hero — handsome, intelligent and brave.

In 1596 he led an attack on Cadiz, Spain's major port. The next year, 1597, the Queen gave him command of the navy. Then she made him Earl Marshal of England, one of the greatest honours she could give.

But Elizabeth and the Earl often quarrelled, and in March 1599 she sent him away to Ireland.

His task was to defeat the Earl of Tyrone's soldiers and regain control of the country. He commanded an army of 16,000 but instead of fighting, the Earl of Essex made peace — against all the Queen's orders. Elizabeth was furious. Immediately the Earl left his army and went back to England. He rode straight to the Queen's palace, and burst into her bedroom. She was not even dressed, but he wanted to explain why he had disobeyed her. As he left her room, the Earl thought their quarrel was over. Soon after he was under arrest.

People said that he had planned to get rid of Elizabeth, and make himself ruler of England.

A *This picture of the Earl of Essex was drawn in 1601.*

B *The Earl of Essex's house.*

For months the Queen could not decide what to do with him. Finally she set him free, on condition that he never went near the palace again. The Earl of Essex was ruined. He was ill and in debt.

C *What he did next is described in this account written by John Stowe in 1615.*

About 10 o'clock on Sunday 8 February, 1601 the Earl of Essex came to London. With him was the Earl of Southampton and many others. They passed Fleet Street and the people of London said that the Queen and the Earl had made friends, and that Her Majesty let him ride in this triumphant way to his house in Seeding Lane.

As he went the people cried, 'God save your Honour.' But at Paul's Cross the Lord Mayor was warned by the Council and by 11 o'clock the city gates were shut and strongly guarded. The Earl kept his course towards Fenchurch and entered the Sheriff of London's house. The Earl went into an armourer's house, wanting ammunition. This was denied him and he went back to Gracechurch Street.

By this time Lord Burghley had arrived and in the Queen's name proclaimed the Earl and all his followers traitors. Then one of the Earl's followers shot a pistol at the Lord. He saw how determined they were and went back to the court which was now double guarded. Many streets were full of empty carts and coaches to stop the Earl getting through.

About 2 o'clock, the earl, who had been left by all his followers, decided to go home. At Ludgate he was turned back by a company of well-armed men, put there by the Bishop of London. The Earl went into Friday Street. Here he felt faint and was given a drink. At his request, the people lifted up the great chain which blocked the street and let him through.

After that he took a boat at Queenshithe and back to his house. At ten o'clock when he saw the **artillery** and the Queen's forces around the house, he gave himself up. This time the Earl of Essex could expect no mercy. Even then the Queen hesitated before ordering his execution.

The Earl of Essex was sent to trial and found guilty of treason. He was beheaded on 25 February 1601 at the Tower of London. But although she had had him executed, Elizabeth continued to wear the ring he had given her, for the rest of her life.

D *The Queen's godson, Sir John Harington, wrote this about the Earl of Essex early in the 17th century.*

In my opinion, thwarted ambition speedily leads on to madness. His speeches to the Queen were not those of a man who had a sound mind in a sound body.

E *The Royal warrant for the execution of the Earl of Essex.*

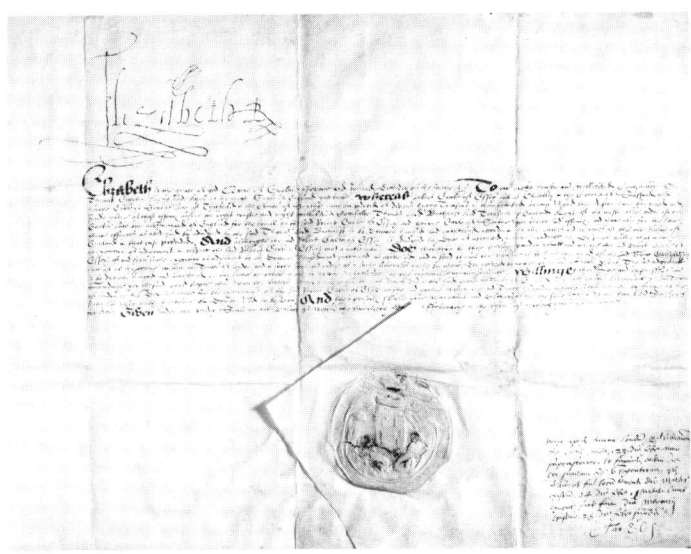

Activities

1. a) Look at source A. What impression do you get of the Earl of Essex from this picture?
   b) Can you tell from this source whether the artist was biased in favour of the Earl, or against him? Give reasons.

2. a) According to source D, why did the Earl of Essex behave as he did?
   b) Why might this not be a reliable source about the Earl?

3. a) Read source C. What did the Lord Mayor and Lord Burghley think the Earl was trying to do?
   b) What questions would you need to ask before you decided if this source was accurate, or not?
   c) You are a newspaper reporter. Think of a headline and in your own words write a report about the Essex Rebellion.

19 Ireland

In England and Wales people accepted Elizabeth as their Queen and obeyed her laws. In Ireland, where she was also Queen, the situation was different.

Here the people were divided into **clans**. Each clan had its own chieftain, or leader, and its own land. Queen Elizabeth thought the land belonged to her.

A *English soldiers fight with Irish cattle raiders.*

B *An Irish cattle raid.*

C *English soldiers return after the fight.*

For years the clans had fought each other, stealing cattle and burning crops. Meanwhile, the English army tried to keep order.

In spite of this, the clans had more in common with each other than they did with England.

The clans shared the same views on religion. They were Catholics. The English were Protestants.

Those chieftains who refused to accept English laws, chose instead to fight. In 1579 the Earl of Desmond led a rebellion by the Fitzgerald clan.

Even more serious was the Ulster Rebellion of 1592. This one, led by Hugh O'Neill, went on for eleven years. Worse still, the King of Spain sent an army to help fight the English.

To Queen Elizabeth, the problem was clear. England was less than 50 miles (80 km) across the sea from Ireland. If she lost control there, England could easily be invaded. In 1598 the O'Neill clan defeated her army for the first time. She could not let it happen again.

D *An Irish chieftain eating dinner.*

Soon after, the Queen sent another 10,000 soldiers to Ireland. This time they were successful. The Spanish army surrendered in 1601. Two years later, the O'Neill clan, surrounded and outnumbered, did the same.

At last Ireland was under England's control, but Queen Elizabeth did not live to see it. She died a week before Hugh O'Neill's surrender.

E *Edmund Spencer wrote this account in 1596. He describes what happened after the Desmond Rebellion, when English soldiers destroyed farm land in southern Ireland.*

Out of every corner of the woods and **glens** they came creeping forward on their hands. Their legs were too weak to carry their weight. They looked like skeletons. They spoke like ghosts crying out of their graves. They ate dead crows, and one another soon after. They even scraped carcasses out of their graves. And if they found a field of watercress or shamrocks they flocked there, as if to a feast. In this war it is true that not many died by the sword. They died because of famine, which they themselves had caused.

F *This is an old Spanish proverb.*

He that England will win, through Ireland he must come in.

Activities

1. Read source F and then read this chapter again. Why do you think the Spanish King sent soldiers to fight in Ireland?

2. a) Read source E. Do you think the writer feels sorry for these people or not?
   b) Why do you think the English army destroyed so much farm land during the 1596 Rebellion?

3. a) Look at sources A–D. Arrange them in the order which you think best tells the story.
   b) Explain what you think is happening in each source.
   c) Describe the armour and weapons of the English soldiers.
   d) What advantages did English soldiers have over Irish soldiers?

Glossary

ale – drink made from malt and flavoured with hops
allegiance – loyalty to a king, queen or government
alliance – an agreement made between countries to help each other
arable – land used to grow crops
artillery – large guns, cannons
assassins – killers
ballad – a type of poem which is sung
belladonna – deadly nightshade: a poisonous plant
broadside – the side of a ship between the bows and the stern, from which its heaviest guns were fired
cauldron – a large pot with a hooped handle used to boil water
clan – a group of people, related by birth, who share a common ancestor
colony – an area where a group of people settle in a new country
contract – a legal agreement
crescent – a curved shape like the new or old moon
excommunicate – to stop someone from taking part in any official church activities
fit – a sudden illness which causes someone to lose control of their body
gallow balke – an iron support for pots and pans
girdle – a belt
glen – a narrow valley
harquebussiers – soldiers armed with an early type of gun
heifer – a young cow
inventory – a detailed list
justices – judges
malt – barley or other type of grain used for brewing
mastiff – a large, powerful dog
midwife – someone who helps a woman give birth
mutilated – badly wounded
oath – a solemn promise
page – a young, male servant
pewter – a metal made from a mixture of tin with lead or other metal
Popish – Roman Catholic
proceedings – process by which disputes are settled according to the law
pulpit – raised platform in a church from which a preacher speaks
Puritan – a Protestant who wanted changes in the Church of England to make it even less like the Roman Catholic Church
quart – two pints, 1.1 litres
quartering – hacking the body of a rebel into four parts
reckons – hooks to support pots over a fire
reliquary – a pouch or box used to hold small religious objects
repentant – feeling sorry for past sins or crimes
rogue – a beggar who pretended to be ill
scolds – nagging women
slanderous – unfair spoken comment by someone about someone else
spit – a thin iron rod on which meat is fixed to roast
spontaneous fracture – a sudden break in a bone
subjects – people who obey a king, queen or government
superstitious – believing in the supernatural
tapestry – a decorative picture made from wool woven on linen
Testament – a religious notebook
theory – a possible explanation for something that has happened
treason – the crime of disobeying or plotting against a ruler
warming pan – a covered pan filled with hot coals, used to warm a bed
woodcut – an illustration in a book made from a wooden engraving

Index

Bothwell, Earl of 10–11
Catholics 4–7, 12–13, 16–17, 28
Children 22–23
Darnley, Lord Henry 10–11
Drake, Sir Francis 25, 30, 32
Dudley, Amy 8–9
Dudley, Lord Robert 8–9
Elizabeth I 4–9, 12, 14–16, 26, 28–32, 36, 38, 44–7
Essex, Earl of 44–45
Farming 18–21
Football 34
Hakluyt, Richard 41
Hariot, Thomas 40
Hawkins, Captain John 24–25
Henry II 6
Hoby, Lady Margaret 7
Hunting 34, 41
Ireland 46–47
Mary I 4, 6
Mary, Queen of Scots 4, 6–7, 10–13, 28–29
Philip II 6, 30–31, 46
Poor Rate 36–37
Protestants 4, 6–7, 16–17
Slavery 24–25
Spanish Armada 30–33
Virginia 38–40
West Indies 25
Women 26–27